Ronnie Corbett's ARMCHAIR GOLF

WITH CLIVE CLARK

WILLOW BOOKS
Collins
8 Grafton Street
London
1986

Willow Books
William Collins & Sons Ltd
London · Glasgow · Sydney · Auckland
Toronto · Johannesburg

First published 1986

BRITISH LIBRARY CATALOGUING IN PUBLICATION DATA

Corbett, Ronnie
Ronnie Corbett's armchair golf.
1. Golf — Anecdotes, facetiae, satire etc
I. Title
II. Clark, Clive
796.352'0207 6V967

ISBN 0 00 218214 9

Photoset in Crown
by V & M Graphics Ltd, Aylesbury, Bucks

Made and printed in Great Britain
by Hazell Watson & Viney Ltd, Aylesbury

CONTENTS

From the Armchair 9

Celebrity Golf 11
- Kenyan catastrophe 11
- Tarby 13
- The drunken president 16

Golfers on Wheels 19
- The million dollar bash 19
- Hunt the shunt 21
- Faulkner's folly 23
- Victorious Von 25

Cashmere Shoes and Alligator Sweaters 29
- Put-down of the year 29
- He who laughs last… 31
- Well qualified for the post 32
- Star struck out 33
- The empire strikes back 34

Henry Longhurst 37
- What? Me, Officer? 38
- Silence is golden 39
- Dropping the brick 40
- Well trained 42
- Jack and Jill 43
- Lift-off 44
- More Longhurst gems 45

Great Golfers 47
- Lee Trevino 47
- Gary Player 49
- Gary Player and Arnold Palmer 50
- Jack Nicklaus and Tom Weiskopf 51
- Byron Nelson 53
- Tommy Bolt 54
- Bobby Cole meets the greats 55
- Sam Snead and Ben Hogan 59
- Ben Hogan 60

Back to the Armchair 61

May I Play Mulligan? 63
Strange goings-on in the olive grove 63
Rained off 65
Flaming cheek 66
Slanderous allegations 67

Caddies 71
One Tooth Jock 71
The water of life 73
In Thomson's footsteps 74
Well travelled 76
Unidentified flying object 77

Cook in the Soup 79
Disaster at La Manga 79
Silent partner 81
The last straw 84

How's It Lying, Clive? 89
The filler's art 90
Quick change 92
Mum's the word 93
Red braces — red faces 94
The sharp end 96

Fluffs, Bumbles and Shanks 97
Not 'another' speech 97
The pro from Milwaukee 99
A journalist's lot 101
Arthur the great 102
I am the greatest 105

Some gems from the Suggestions Books 107

Mountain Rules - Mount Mitchell 113

Richmond Golf Club 117
Temporary Rules 1940 117

Finally, From the Armchair 119

FROM THE ARMCHAIR

I'd like, if I may, to tell you a brand new golf joke, which has never been heard before. Actually, when I say it's never been heard before, that's not entirely true. Let's be honest — this joke is so old it was found buried with the Dead Sea Scrolls. Along with the comedian who told it. It actually dates back to 256 BC which, as scholars of Ancient Egypt will know, was the year of the famous wild-cat strike by the amalgamated union of eunuchs and allied sopranos over a dispute regarding severance pay.

Incidentally, I would like to thank all those people who have written in over the years suggesting what I might do with my act. And particularly those of you who sent diagrams.

I'm delighted to say that offers of work have been flooding in. Recently, I was invited to go on a Round the World Golfing Cruise to entertain members of the Flat Earth Golfing Society.

Then I was invited to make a very important after-dinner speech at Sunningdale Golf Club. I said, 'Do you want me to be funny?' And they said, 'No, just be yourself.'

Arnold Palmer was on *World At One* today. When asked if he felt he could win another Open Championship, he said that nothing was impossible though he admitted he'd never tried cancelling a Reader's Digest subscription.

No, no ... I seem to have wandered off the main point again. I was going to tell you this golf story about a friend of mine in the Doldrums. Now, don't ask me which part of the Doldrums ... I think it was the northern part. Anyway, he used to enjoy going to the golf club but it's very cold in that part of the country and the club's heating system was a bit temperamental. There were times when it snowed in the gent's airing cupboard ... and the rising damp was so bad, the mice were often seen punting around on mouse traps.

Actually, I'm digressing ... the point was that this friend of mine forgot their wedding anniversary. Their anniversary was on the 4th of April. Now, he should have remembered that date clearly — it's the one day of the year when there isn't a sale on at Allied Carpets.

Anyway, he came downstairs in the morning and she was expecting

the usual flowers and chocolates to be showered on her, but there was nothing and he went off to the office, leaving her empty-handed.

Understandably, she was extremely upset. Now there had always been this promise between them throughout their married life regarding the chest at the bottom of their bed — it was strictly forbidden for her to open it as it had always been his little private domain.

However, on this particular occasion she was so very upset at his having obviously forgotten their anniversary, that she opened the chest. In it, she was puzzled to find four golf balls and £800.

When he eventually arrived home that evening, he was laden with flowers, perfume and chocolates and she immediately admitted her guilt. 'I'm sorry, my darling, I've behaved very badly and have selfishly opened the chest. But tell me, why are you keeping four golf balls, and what is the £800 for?'

'All right, my dear,' said the husband. 'I might as well tell you. Every time I was unfaithful to you during our marriage I placed one golf ball in the chest.'

'Oh, well,' she said, 'four times in twenty-seven years of marriage is not too bad. But what about the £800?'

'Well, every time I collected a dozen golf balls, I sold them for £10.'

CELEBRITY GOLF

Kenyan catastrophe

The Variety Club of Great Britain used to organise a tremendous trip to Kenya in aid of Joytown, a crippled children's home in Nairobi. It was run in conjunction with the Kenyan Open and the celebrities performed at a very grand Gala Dinner. It was a great favourite with the celebrities and everyone used to support it from Jimmy Tarbuck to Bobby Charlton, from Eric Sykes to Henry Cooper.

First treat on arrival in Nairobi was a three-day trip to the Game Reserve. That was the good news. The bad news was that you were taken there by a Dakota of 1942 vintage. It looked like one of those cardboard cut-out efforts – the sort that keels over on its side when you remove the chocks. Dickie Henderson sat in the back, on the grounds that he'd never heard of a plane backing into a mountain. Anyway, we had a great trip and landed somewhere near the airstrip of Keekorok.

We were taken for a splendid lunch at the residential game lodge. That was the good news. The bad news was that we were staying in the tents a mile down the road. Now, I don't know how you feel about wild boar and wildebeest whistling past your tent door throughout the night, but frankly it doesn't do very much for me.

A sleepless night was followed by an early morning shower. You have this in something resembling a Punch and Judy tent and your steward fills the rusty bucket above your head. You then pull a chain and the primitive

shower bursts into action. Not so good, though, when you're halfway through and find there's a monkey having a piddle in your bucket. This is not an infrequent occurrence. Not everyone smells sweet at breakfast.

The one trouble with Kenya is that particularly nasty stomach upsets can run rampant throughout a stay. These were christened 'the Kenya two-step' by Dickie Henderson. Few escape, and on this trip the first sufferers were Eric Sykes and Sir John's wife, Lady Mills.

Early that morning we were taken to the Masai village. The Masai people put rings around their necks to make them longer. When we arrived — what a smell! The Masai build their round houses from cow cake and mud; and the cows often live with them in their huts. It was like a zoo for flies.

Eric, who had done nothing for two days except run to the smallest room, took one look at these unusual buildings and said, swiping at the flies, 'If I'd only come here a day or two earlier, I could have finished off their roof for them.'

Putting her arm around Eric's shoulder, Lady Mills added, 'Together, Eric, we could have built a high rise!'

Tarby

James Tarbuck Esq was once commissioned to go to Australia. Anyone who has been there will know just what an awful journey it is ... about thirty hours by plane.

Arriving in Sydney, Jimmy clambered down the steps, a little the worse for wear. It was not the best time to get a microphone stuffed under your nose — but a TV news crew was waiting.

The caustic Aussie interviewer demanded, 'You're supposed to be a very funny man. Make me laugh.'

Tarbuck, who is not known for slowness off the mark, retorted, 'Lend me your jacket and we can all have a laugh.'

There's probably nobody in show business who enjoys golf more than Jimmy Tarbuck. He has worked very hard at the game and enjoys the fruits of practice, hence his 5 handicap. His competitive nature doesn't do any harm either.

If you meet him walking into the London Weekend Television recording studios, or nipping through the stage door at Her Majesty's, and ask him where he'd prefer to be, you would probably get a longish list.

Tarby likes the nice weather and the great courses. Put him on the Monterey Peninsula, with courses such as Pebble Beach, Spyglass Hill and Cypress Point, and that would be Heaven. The Sunningdales, Wentworths and Berkshires are also close to his heart. And in Marbella and Portugal he is a regular.

Jimmy is a great supporter and a respecter of the traditions of this fascinating game. Going round the course, he will usually spin you a line with a twinkle in the eye:

'Did you see that Irish farm lad who went to the Kerry Fair? And there was a gypsy there, holding a large egg.

"What's that," said the farmhand.

"It's a greyhound's egg," said the gypsy.

"Is it after being for sale?"

"It's yours for £10," said the gypsy.

"I'll take it."

So off goes the farmhand back to the farm with his mate and they are going down the hill to the farm when the egg falls out of his hand and rolls

off down the hill. Well, they are off after it but before they can catch it, it hits a large boulder and is smashed to pieces.

The rabbit that was under the boulder came shooting out, covered in yoke.

"Look at it go," said the excited Irishman, "And it's only a pup."'

Tarby ran a very successful quiz show produced by Yorkshire Television, called *Winner Takes All*. It ran for six years. But the viewers saw only the edited version — not everything that went on in the studio. Tarby was full of hilarious stories about the bits they cut out...

When the programme began, he introduced the guests, 'This is Arthur. This is Robert. Good luck to both of you, you have £50.' Whatever happened — however stupid the answers were — Jimmy was not allowed to laugh.

They had one fellow who bet £50 on who wrote *The Thirty-Nine Steps*. He pressed 'Victor Sylvester'. Another time, Jimmy asked a posh lady from Kensington, 'Could you name me four animals from Africa?' After a moment's thought, she replied, 'Three lions and a giraffe.'

He also had an old lady on the show who was a senior citizen. Jimmy asked, 'For £1000, who was the first man?'

'Oh no,' she replied. 'I wouldn't tell you for £5000.'

Jimmy is a very spontaneous comedian. One of his best lines came during his hearing for being over the limit. The Judge gravely asked, 'Mr Tarbuck, before I pass sentence, do you have anything to say for yourself?'

'Yes, Your Honour,' said Jimmy. 'Could I have a lift home?' The Court erupted!

Many years ago, there was a very large pro-am at Southport, which was sponsored by Texaco.

All the top golfers had come down from the Player Classic at Turnberry. The celebrity list was a mile long with names like Bing Crosby, Max Bygraves, Eric Sykes, Henry Cooper and Sean Connery. It was quite a turnout.

Jimmy Tarbuck was having dinner with Henry Cooper and Eric Sykes in the Prince of Wales Hotel when a man carrying a rugby ball came up to their table and, rudely interrupting the dinner, said, 'Here Jimmy, sign my ball.'

Tarbuck obligingly signed the gentleman's ball, adding: 'For someone suffering from such a severe affliction, how could I possibly refuse.'

The drunken president

Foster Brookes, the American comedian who does the best drunk act you've ever seen, used to come over for the Bob Hope tournament. The first year he came to Britain he was unknown over here, even though he is a big star in the States.

On the night of the gala dinner at Grosvenor House, Hope, for a joke, introduced Brookes as the President of the United States Golf Association, a highly-respected position.

Weaving between the dinner tables at Grosvenor House, Brookes staggered on to the stage. Looking extremely embarrassed, apologetic and plastered, he said, 'I must apologise to you for appearing before you in this condition. However, before you condemn me too soon, I feel in all fairness to myself, I must say I have a very good reason for being loaded tonight — I've been drinking all day!

'I became involved with golf a number of years ago when Mr H-H-o-... er ... Bob, asked me if I would play golf in his tourna-tourn- ... er ... contest, in Palm Springs, California, and I told him, I said, "Bob ... I don't play golf." He said, "It doesn't matter, we would love to have you; we'd love to have you come down and play and it doesn't matter how you score. No matter how you play the game, you still have the chance to win a very nice prize." And so I went down to Palm Springs and they showed me the courtesy of letting me hit first. So I put one of those little sticks in the ground and I put a ball on it and I swung at it and it went way out in the field there, and I was rather proud of myself at being able to hit the ball.

'I stepped down off the mound and a gentleman walked up and tapped me on the shoulder and said, "Mr Brookes, would you like a caddie?" I thought I'd won a car! He finally explained to me that a caddie was a young man who went around with you and would help you find the ball if you knocked it in the woods or in the rough. I know that Bob told everyone that I had never played golf before, because they started me off with two dozen brand new golf balls and when I got to the 8th tee I didn't have any balls left! I had lost two of them in the ball washer! I remember at one particular spot on the golf course I wanted to try to make them think I was not completely ignorant of the game. I looked at the ball and then I looked off towards the green and back at the ball like I knew what I was going to do, and I said to the caddie, "Young man, d'ya think I can get home from here with a little 4-iron?" He said, "I don't even know where you live!"

'When I realised I didn't have any balls left, I looked at my caddie and I said, "Boy, I'm telling you what, you gotta be the worst caddie in the whole world." He looked at me and said, "I don't think so, Mr Brookes, that would be too much of a coincidence!"'

Quote
'Golf really is a stupid game.'
'You're absolutely right. I'm sure glad I don't have to play again until tomorrow.'

GOLFERS ON WHEELS

The million dollar bash

Mrs H, having enjoyed a particularly good Sunday lunch at her local golf club, went to collect her Honda Prelude Automatic from the car park. Normally, this would have been a somewhat mundane procedure. It was, until a slight lapse caused her to confuse the brake and accelerator!

On her first strike, she hit a BMW, a Ford Escort and a Ford Granada. She removed only part of the front bumper and nearside from the BMW. The Ford Escort was a sadder case. It belonged to a very senior member. He was seventy-three years old, and this was the first new car he had ever owned. The vehicle had been delivered only some three days before, and

had less than 200 miles on the clock. Though repairable, it sustained severe rear-end damage, as did the Granada, which was walloped with such force it was shunted through a perimeter fence. That stopped Mrs H for the moment.

It was an incredible stroke of luck, though, that the only witness to the accident was former World Champion racing driver James Hunt. He'd just finished his round.

James had had the odd shunt or two during his career. Who better to give advice?

'Stick it into reverse and ease it back gently,' said James, giving Mrs H the worst possible advice.

Mrs H followed the instructions to the letter and found 'R'. She eased the car back. The problem is that when you confuse the brake pedal and the accelerator, the harder you 'brake' the more you accelerate, the more you 'brake'...

Before you could say, 'Jack Flash', she was off at 100 miles per hour in reverse and would have made an unscheduled visit to the pro's shop had she not first hit a Mercedes Sports. Then she panicked.

Cranking the gear lever back into 'Drive' and with her foot flat on the floorboards, she was off again on her third strike.

It was at this point that her husband, with the King Charles spaniel, rounded the corner to join the amazed James Hunt. They were both now right in the firing line and the strike car was bearing down on them at full tilt!

Was Hunt, who had survived at least a hundred Grands Prix, about to cop it in the car park? A sprightly leap saved the day. He almost set another world record as he sailed over the remains of the fence to the safety of a nearby garden.

Mrs H's husband, a heavy man, was rooted to the spot. She missed him by inches. The King Charles was less fortunate and Mr H was left holding only a foot or so of lead.

Mrs H was now at full throttle as she headed for the big game in the bottom car park.

Lord King's gleaming Bentley was first in line. Mrs H took out his front wing, bumper and headlights. Still accelerating, she just spared the Aston Martin, but hit the Mercedes 500 SEC head on. That *finally* stopped her!

Was it a local caddie? Who knows. But William Hickey had a field day the following morning. The bill came to a tidy sum in excess of £45,000!

Quote from Mr H: 'I don't know what all the fuss is about. This sort of thing happens every day on the motorways.'

Hunt the shunt

Although James Hunt, often seen on the fairways with Oscar the Alsatian who has A levels in ball finding, survived the Mrs H escapade he has had a bit of bad luck on the motorways himself. I suppose that it's fair to say that Formula One drivers have different ideas about how to drive when not on the race track. Some are slow — some just go! They don't trust amateurs and anyway they reckon the one-way system at Brands is a far safer road to travel. That was always Graham Hill's theory.

Others, however, use the accelerator fairly freely. James Hunt was bombing down the A3, not doing anything serious — just a steady 90 miles per hour, which caught the attention of the law. Spotting them in the mirror, James slowed to an acceptable speed. They followed for a mile or so, then disappeared up an exit ramp. As James watched them disappear, his foot went down again. What he didn't realise was that they'd gone up the exit ramp and down the entry ramp and were now steaming up behind him with their blue light working overtime.

Being 150 yards or so ahead, James saw no reason not to use a few of his professional skills. These, plus the help of a Ford Mustang and all did not look lost.

'Better not risk a road block,' thought the cunning Hunt. 'I'll outdrive them down the country lanes.'

This he did with comparative ease, even though the boys in blue were in devastating form.

Then James had a bit of bad luck. Taking a bend, he braked late, hit a nasty patch of mud from a local farmer's field, and lost the back end. The car's rear slewed into the verge. But, like a true pro, James quickly had it under control.

His second bit of bad luck happened when he came into a small village and the lights were red. To compound his embarrassment, a Panda car was sitting on the adjacent corner. Working on the theory that 'it's better not to hang about in situations like these,' he shot the lights. Now the second Panda car had joined the chase.

After a further couple of miles, James had reached the safety of a friend's house and slid the Mustang into the double garage. After a relaxing cup of tea, he went out to inspect the damage. Apart from a very minor 'biff' incurred when he thumped the kerb, the only other damage was a missing hub cap. Taking his mate's Mini, he returned to the bend where he had lost the back end and, to his amazement, not only found the missing hub cap, but there was a large hole in the hedge and sitting in the field was a rather sad-looking Panda car. They had gone round the corner with less agility than the World Champion!

Faulkner's folly

Max Faulkner was always one of my favourite characters in golf. That craggy face, slicked-back hair and coloured wardrobe ... the plus-twos (often pink or some equally outrageous colour), the wide robot-like stance ... the upright posture, knees well bent, and that deliberate backswing. 'I say, Governor!' Max would say. 'You've got to take it back like a waiter with a tray. You've got to get that right elbow in the correct position at the top.' He was quite a teacher, and to hell with anyone else's theories!

Max also had a liking for cars. He seldom held back and collected a fair bit of automobile exotica. Not that all his acquisitions had a smooth ride. I remember him once getting into trouble with the law for removing a traffic bollard with his Bentley. Anyone who knows Max will confirm that he was not exactly the shy, retiring type. In Court, he did his case no good at all when he told the Judge, 'You look more like a broken-down bookie, Governor.'

His first E-type came to grief when, late one night on a wet Sussex lane, he lost control of it on a right-hand bend. He was doing no mean speed and as the car hit the kerb it took off, cleared the hedge, soared over a narrow valley and he got a plugged lie on the adjacent bank.

'I didn't know what was going on, Governor. All I could see were tree tops going past.'

He was very lucky. The car had somersaulted several times and landed upside down, flattening the roof. Max dug his way out of the back window. Shaken and cut, he eventually found a farm.

'When they opened the door, I swear they thought Christopher Lee's accomplice had turned up,' said the incorrigible Faulkner.

So Max had had a few nasty moments behind the wheel, but perhaps the one that frightened him most happened as he was returning home from a tournament in Surrey. He was in a low sports car when the accident occurred. Max drove on to the nearest telephone box and called his friend, David Wickins, who is Chairman of British Car Auctions and happened to be the Honorary Chief Constable of Surrey Police at the time.

'I've done it now,' croaked Max down the phone. 'I don't know how many I've got.'

'What are you talking about?' asked Wickins. 'It's 2 o'clock in the morning.'

'I know,' persisted Max. 'But I must have run at least a dozen of them down. There's blood and guts all over the place.'

Wickins ascertained that Max was hiding behind a garage on the A3. 'Stay there,' he said. 'I'll be right down.'

Wickins was there in under fifteen minutes. He found Max in an awful state, still splattered in blood.

'Get your clothes off,' said Wickins, grabbing the garage's hose.

He hosed Max down, wrapped him up in some old sacks that were lying around, and put him in his car.

'We'd better go back and see what damage you've done.'

'Might have been a whole platoon of them, Governor,' said Faulkner, still shaking.

The accident wasn't quite as serious as Max had thought. Wickins discovered the sorry remains of a cow on the side of the road.

'What a horrible thing,' said Max. 'But, thank goodness, I thought I'd got a whole regiment.'

Victorious Von

Norman von Nida was the first of the great Australian players to hit Britain just after the War. In the late 1940s he and Dai Rees were sweeping all before them. In fact, in 1947 von Nida played with such gusto that he had seven tour victories, three of them after play-offs with the most illustrious golfers of the day: Henry Cotton, Flory van Donck and Dai Rees. It will appeal to those with long memories to ponder that while the likes of Ballesteros, Faldo and Langer are competing in events like the St Mellion Timeshare Tournament Players Championship and the Compagnie de Chauffe Cannes Open, von Nida was winning events with less salubrious titles that sadly no longer exist. His victories included such tournaments as the Spalding, North British, Yorkshire Evening News and the Lotus.

'The Von', as he was affectionately called, was very small, always wore a beret, had a quick tongue, a quick wit and a quicker temper. All these attributes actually concealed a heart of gold beneath a craggy exterior.

He drove consistently, though he seldom went under 65 and seemingly never did more than 70. The same was true of his driving on the road. He never went over 70 and certainly didn't do much under it. I think I do him no injustice when I say his style of driving was more suited to a Sherman tank! In town, his speed was reduced to a consistent 45; never over, seldom under. The driver's window was always down, not for the sake of letting cool air in, more for letting hot air out. Any motorist or pedestrian who dared to impede von Nida's course caught the wrath and fire of The Von, and quaint old Australian words were hurled in their direction. Should a pedestrian so much as threaten to step from the kerb, he would most certainly be blasted back to the safety of the pavement. Sooner or later, you felt, an irate motorist was going to punch the little man – but it never happened. His verbal lashings were always directed with total and commanding authority.

Perhaps his finest moment, though, was driving back to his lovely house (called 'Sunningdale') at Maroubra Beach, just outside Sydney. He was not overly pleased at his 73 round at the Manly Golf Club. In Australia there is a rule of the road that you always give way to vehicles coming from your right, regardless of whether you are on the major road or not.

Norman had got up a fair amount of steam as he was approaching an intersection. Unfortunately, a packed double-decker bus was approaching from the right. Undeterred, Norman went for the crossing. The bus did likewise. Amid a flurry of braking, skidding and burning rubber, both vehicles came to a stop within inches of each other. Norman's window was down, but the irate crew-cutted Sydney bus driver already had his head out of his window and was shrieking at Norman.

'Haven't you got any bloody brains?' he yelled.

Norman, who was seldom lost for an answer, countered, 'Got any bloody brains, mate? Why do you think I'm driving a Jaguar and you're driving a bus!'

I think that was a clear cut case of game, set and match, Mr von Nida!

Quote

Bolt on Bolt: 'Sure I'm even-tempered on the course. I stay mad all the time.'

CASHMERE SHOES AND ALLIGATOR SWEATERS

Put-down of the year

Lord Matthews, the vice-chairman of Trafalgar House and the Cunard Shipping Line, had agreed to play with a friend of a friend. You might find him a little over the top,' said Matthews' friend. 'But he's all right really.' Lord Matthews himself is a kindly, modest man who tends not to flaunt his possessions.

The friend's friend arrived, parking his gleaming Ferrari halfway up the clubhouse steps.

'Glad to meet you,' said his Lordship. 'Like your shoes.'

'Ah ... best alligator,' replied the friend's friend. 'Handmade by Maxwells, only £500. A steal.'

The game commenced.

'Did you drive over?' asked Lord Matthews.

'Yes. You probably noticed my Ferrari near the members' entrance, but I like my Lagonda better. Had to sell the Spirit – found the ride a bit spongey.'

In no time at all, he'd recited the names of all twelve golf clubs of which he was a member.

The chat continued. And, of course, he played golf all the time with Sean, Tarby and Bruce, and even with Glen Campbell and James Garner when he visited the States.

'Travel quite a lot?' inquired the ever-modest Lord Matthews.

'Oh yes. Have a five-bedroomed apartment just outside Cannes and a penthouse in Marbella. The wife prefers Marbella because our boat is moored in Puerto Banus. She's a beauty you know ... an 85-foot luxury ten-berth cruiser. She's done out like you wouldn't believe.' Chuckling, he added, 'Even has gold-plated fittings. She's called *Midas I.* I expect, though, you're the sort of man who would have a boat yourself'.

'Oh, yes,' said Matthews.

'And what's yours called?'

'You may have heard of it...The *QE2.*'

He who laughs last...

John Tethington is almost seventy, is a member of several well-known London golf clubs and maintains a 6 handicap. He's a very precise man and drives a large Mercedes Saloon, which he bought some five years ago.

He lives close to Sloane Square, so parking is never easy, but one day, after a long search, he had found a space and was about to park. He pulled past the vacant spot and was just on the point of reversing when a young chap in a sports car drove straight into his place.

Tethington was fuming and the young man did nothing to ease matters by jumping out of his car, locking the door and saying, 'You've got to be young to do that!'

Tethington, a man who didn't like being beaten at golf or anything else, exploded.

Incensed, he rammed his gearbox into reverse and smashed into the little sports car, shunting it halfway up the pavement.

Leaning out of his window triumphantly, Tethington looked the young man straight in the eye and said, 'And you've got to be wealthy to do that!'

Well qualified for the post

The committee of a well-known Scottish golf club advertised for an Assistant Secretary.

A very snobbish old Major replied, recommending a certain young man for the job.

The Major wrote, 'Mr Blake is a first-class young man. He is the son of Major Blake, the grandson of General Blake, the cousin of Sir Reginald Blake, the nephew of Lord Blake, and he is otherwise well-connected.'

The committee replied, 'Thank you very much for your letter of recommendation concerning Mr Blake. We must point out, though, that we require him for tending to the needs of our members, and not for breeding purposes.'

Quote
First prize for diplomacy to the journalist who, describing the winning putt of the One-Armed Championship, wrote: 'And he grabbed his opportunity with both hands.'

Star struck out

There was a card-signing incident, or rather lack of, a few years ago, involving Greg Norman at the Hong Kong Open. Greg opened with a fine 67 around the par-72 Royal Hong Kong Golf Course. He was just one stroke behind Graham Marsh. It was then discovered that Greg had not signed his card. It would have been a catastrophic state of affairs if the star of the event had been disqualified. Someone spotted the omission and a signature from Greg was hastily acquired. A slight leniency in application of the rules, perhaps.

I remember discussing the event with Peter Alliss. 'It reminds me,' he said, 'of the time when a good friend of W.G. Grace invited the great man to lead a team against his local village cricket club. Grace opened the batting. To the amazement of everyone, the village smithy pounded down the wicket and removed Grace's leg stump with his first ball.

'Grace retrieved the stump and bails, replaced them in their original position, took up his stance once more and yelled down the pitch, ... "They've come to watch me bat, not you bowl!"...'

The empire strikes back

Like most golfers, I've always clung tenaciously to the old ways. Yards, feet, inches — what's wrong with them? Metres, millimetres — rubbish, that's what I say. I'm glad to say Peter Alliss thinks so too — and here's how he upheld the Empire at the 1979 Australian Open.

The Open was at the Metropolitan Club, a very fine tree-lined course on the outskirts of Melbourne. Australia had just gone metric and as the Head of Sport was also Deputy Commissioner of Weights and Measures, the commentary team was told all distances were to be called in metres and centimetres.

Now just imagine having to say, 'And it's Arnold Palmer putting for a birdie on the 17th from 5.5 metres... Oh, what a shame - it only just missed the hole by 5 millimetres and has gone 90 centimetres past.'

Alliss dismissed this imposition as 'hooey'. To Peter, golf was, and always will be, a game of yards, feet and inches.

'But Peter,' insisted the desperate producer, 'you are not to use Imperial measures.'

If there's one thing Peter doesn't like, it's being defeated. He sat there waiting to go on the air. Smokey Robertson, the Aussie presenter, got the show on the road with a brisk, 'Good day, golfers' ... and handed over to Peter Thomson who did the first stint.

'Right, stop talking, Peter,' instructed the producer. 'I want to bring in the other Peter. And Peter – NO Imperial!'

Alliss took over the commentary with his usual style. There was no action, but he filled beautifully. Then Kel Nagle came on to the screen. 'So,' said Peter, 'it's one of Australia's favourites – Kel Nagle – with a putt of near enough *five paces*.' He didn't refer to metric all afternoon!

Quote
W. C. Fields, having made a fresh air stroke: 'I want to tell yer... it was one of my better shots.'

HENRY LONGHURST

Sadly Henry Longhurst's death in 1978 was a great loss to golf writing and commentary. Peter Alliss and he were great buddies. Latterly they used to fly to the States together to work for the American Broadcasting Company. Henry was in his late sixties then and used to marvel at the high-tech state of television and the fact that he often got a ride on Concorde.

Peter Alliss admits: 'They were wonderful days and Henry used to refer to me as his "minder".' Peter was so fond of Henry that when he died Peter bought his old American Ford Mustang car and had it renovated. He also named his youngest child after him.

It always amuses me, though, when golfers try to compare Peter Alliss's and Henry Longhurst's commentaries. They both have a wealth of supporters and admirers, but it's like trying to compare Kevin Keegan with Sir Stanley Matthews, or a Ferrari with a Rolls. The styles and performances are different, but the results are great!

What? Me, Officer?

Longhurst the journalist was never a reporter. He was a writer. As a television commentator, he had the gift of a splendid voice, a great turn of phrase, and total economy of words.

It was always said he enjoyed the odd tipple. And the story goes that having enjoyed a particularly good lunch in Edinburgh on his way up to Gleneagles, Henry was stopped by the police. As the officer poked his head into Henry's car, he said sternly, 'You're drunk.' Henry, to his eternal credit, supposedly replied, 'Thank God for that – I thought my steering had gone!'

Silence is golden

Henry was, in fact, the man who brought the 'silence' to American sports broadcasts. He used to commentate at the 16th at Augusta in the US Masters. This beautiful hole over the water is a par-3 measuring 180 yards. It is also the hole where a Gary Player fan once yelled, 'Gary, I want you to know how much we love you,' and then belly-flopped to join the turtles that frequent that particular lake.

An example of Henry's economy was on a day when Palmer was going well. He came to the 16th with a long snaking putt of 20 yards or so up and across the green. The pin was back right on a small ledge.

As the picture changed from another hole to show 'The General' surveying his line, Longhurst said, 'And here is the great man.' That was it.

Palmer continued lining up, hitched his slacks, got set over the ball. It was almost a minute since Henry had said anything. But the pictures were doing the talking.

Just before Arnold struck the putt, Henry endorsed, 'So it's Palmer for a 2.' The ball raced along the bottom plateau, mounted the bank, took the swing and bolted into the hole. The gallery went mad. And Henry let them and the viewers savour the moment. It wasn't until all was quiet again that Henry did his summing up, 'Well, there you have it.'

Dropping the brick

Television has come a long way since the early days of Longhurst. In his later days of broadcasting, Henry always confessed to being amazed that 'the thing' ever got on the air at all. He looked at the sophisticated commentary box with its miles and miles of cable, with screens, computers and contraptions and just shook his head in disbelief.

When Henry started in television, the commentary box was a very basic affair – a tower and a ladder. The scoring system was a piece of

paper carried by a runner. In the open BBC tower, standard issue was a collapsible table, a chair, and a brick to hold down your notes!

I think I'm right in saying that the 1964 World Match Play at Wentworth was one of the first televised events outside the Open. It was Piccadilly's inaugural event.

Longhurst had had a good week and the final was between Arnold Palmer and Neil Coles.

Henry's tower was by the 15th green. A scoring runner arrived just as Arnie's Army was swarming towards the green. The General burst through to acknowledge the now routine tumultuous applause. The runner placed his notes on Henry's desk. But Henry was a little slow with the brick – a gust of wind caught the notes and they fluttered over the heads of the gallery and on to the edge of the green.

Arnold was just lining up his particularly difficult 45-foot downhill putt. Unfortunately, the paper caught his eye. He strode over and picked it up. Scrawled across the offending paper was, 'Arnold Palmer has just three-putted the last two greens.' Glaring up at Henry, Arnold returned to his ball, lined up the tricky down-hiller, hitched his slacks and proceeded to putt. It was a beauty – the pace of the green gathered the ball, which came to rest inches from the hole. Coles conceded and Palmer, never short of humour, looked up at Henry, smiled and gave him a sign to indicate that he had just two-putted. Longhurst chuckled. (He knew what The General meant!)

Well trained

Longhurst was a man who had the ability to talk about a brick for half an hour and make it sound the most interesting object you'd hear of in years.

His television commentaries were famous for the bits he interjected into the programme when there was no action to report.

Many years ago, he was commentating on an international match at St Andrews. The American involved in the match was trailing badly as the producer cut to a pictorial shot of an advancing train.

'And there,' said Henry 'is the 3.25 from Dundee. I can even see its number – 3,3,4,4,3.'

And as the producer cut back to the golf, Henry added, 'And if the American had started that way, it would have been a damned less boring match.'

Jack and Jill

Henry Longhurst used to live in the Hassocks, Sussex. He had a home on the top of the hill which had two windmills. One was called Jack and the other Jill.

Film impresario Nat Cohen once moved in to do some location work. I can't remember the title of the film, but it was a thriller involving Michael Caine.

The windmills were in total disrepair and, as I remember it, Henry's 'fee' for the shoot was to be the renovation of one of them.

Sail-making experts, plasterers and stone-masons appeared on site. By the time they had finished with it, the windmill was unrecognisable.

The 'takes' were finished. I think someone was murdered in the plot. Someone else fell out of the window and broke a leg – that was not in the plot.

The problem now was that Henry had one windmill that was in perfect working order, and one that was not.

Some bright spark once asked Henry, 'How come only one of the windmills' sails go round?'

Henry eyed the man sternly and replied, 'Because there's only enough wind for one of them!'

Lift-off

When the Open was at Carnoustie in 1968, most of the top players and personalities stayed in the Bruce Hotel.

It was a very old, but comfortable, hotel that is no longer with us. Just inside the foyer, past the porter's desk, was a wooden telephone kiosk, but there hadn't been a phone in it for years.

On the first morning of the Championship, a friend of Longhurst's noticed Henry standing in the kiosk. He had been there about a minute. Eventually, his friend's curiosity got the better of him.

He strolled over and asked, 'What are you doing in there, Henry?'

Henry stuffily replied, 'I thought it was a damned lift!'

More Longhurst gems

y man, it's time for desperate measures,' said Henry to the waiter. 'Bring me three.'

Henry was once tackled by someone he did not approve of, regarding a small egg-stain that appeared on his Cambridge college tie.

'Ah well, it will just have to go back to the cleaners,' said Henry. 'And tell me, is that your old school tie, or just your own unfortunate choice?'

Brigadier Peter Wreford-Brown, one of Henry's best friends, gave the address at the great commentator's memorial service. 'Henry would not have approved of this service,' said the Brigadier. 'He would have said it was taking up perfectly good drinking time!'

Quote
Tommy Bolt: 'There's nothing unusual about long hitters. The woods are full of them.'

GREAT GOLFERS

Lee Trevino

I was once travelling in a lift with Lee Trevino following a pro-am. We were accompanied in the lift by a rather large well-endowed lady and unfortunately Lee accidentally bumped her rounded bosom with his elbow.

'I'm sorry – so very sorry, Madam,' said Lee, continuing in his usual charming way, 'but I know that if your heart is as soft as your bosom, you'll forgive me.'

'If the rest of your body is as hard as your elbow,' said the lady with a glint in her eye, 'my room number is 317.'

Gary Player

Gary Player was once approached by a blind friend who is a keen golfer. His caddie would point him in the right direction on long shots and ring a bell by the hole for the putts. Remarkably, his handicap was 14.

'When are we going to play that match, Gary?'

'Which match was that?' inquired Gary.

'Our challenge for $1000.'

'Well, how many shots do you get?' asked Gary.

'Level,' came the reply.

'And what are the conditions of this match?'

'My course at midnight!'

Gary Player and Arnold Palmer

Gary Player recalls the days of 'The Big Three'.

'Players suddenly became conscious of the need to determine the exact direction of the wind by hurling bits of grass into the air. But not Arnie.' quipped Player. 'He used to pluck a couple of hairs off his chest and toss those to the winds!'

Arnie and Gary are great rivals and buddies. Gary, though, never likes carrying loose change around in his pockets. He would frequently ask Arnie or any of his other travelling companions for a couple of dollars to tip the porter. Once, Arnie confided to one of Gary's closest friends, George Blumberg, 'I don't mind, but Gary must owe me $100.'

'Really?' said George. 'I'll speak to him.'

George approached Gary and explained.

'You know, George,' said Gary, 'I didn't realise I owed Arnold that much. Could you lend me $100?'

Jack Nicklaus and Tom Weiskopf

Nicklaus and Weiskopf were playing a practice round before the 1975 Open at Carnoustie, one of the most difficult courses ever to be included on the Open rota.

They got to the fairway on the 2nd. 'We'd like to join you,' hailed Jack Newton from the tee. The 'we' was Jack and his buddy, John O'Leary.

The four was duly made up. According to Tom, Jack never likes to gamble on practice rounds. Also according to Tom, Jack seldom plays particularly well in practice.

'Let's have a few bob on it,' announced Newt.

Jack declined.

'You guys frightened of O'Leary and me?' persisted Newton.

Eventually, Tom and Jack decided they'd had enough from the youngsters and the match was on for £20 corners and automatic £20 presses every time a hole changed hands.

'I've never seen Jack play better,' exclaimed Tom. 'For the last fourteen holes we had thirteen birdies. But an extraordinary thing happened at the par-3 8th. We all hit good shots and mine never left the pin. Out of a thousand-or-so-strong gallery, only my shot drew the slightest ripple of applause. When we got up to the green, there were only three balls. "Yours is in the hole," a disinterested spectator said to me.'

Tom looked in the hole and to his amazement and delight, there was his ball. He'd holed in one.

A puzzled Nicklaus turned to the gallery and said, 'He's holed in one. I can't believe there was so little applause.'

A canny Scot, astride his shooting stick at the front of the gallery, replied, 'Aye. It's only a practice round!'

Byron Nelson

Byron Nelson was not a player who liked to give any information away. When he hit an iron-shot and his opponent tried to catch a sneaky look of his club, Byron responded by putting the head of the club into his trouser pocket.

It was said that one time when Nelson was practising with a 2-iron, he hit his caddie.

'You must have been an unbelievably accurate long-iron player, Mr Nelson,' said an enthusiastic fan.

'Sure was,' said Byron. 'I hit him another six times before he got up.'

Tommy Bolt

Tommy Bolt was known in the trade as 'Thunder Bolt'. His club-throwing was legendary. He once threw a club into a lake in Palm Springs and had to pay a diver £100 to pluck his favourite wedge from the depths. Some writers called him the Vesuvius of the golf tour.

Bolt, though, always protested his innocence. 'You see here. It's my face. I've got this big square jaw. And my ruddy complexion and all. And I never look happy. You take these smiley, talcum-powdered, baby-faced, flippy-wristed college boys they got on tour today and it just don't show when they get mad.'

Tom was once heard to call on the Lord when his ball got buried under the face of a bunker. 'And don't send your Son down. This is a man's job.'

One of the most well-known stories about Tommy Bolt has him on the 18th growling at his caddie – 'Caddie, what club is it?'

'It's a 9-iron.'

'Nine-iron, my foot. We've 200 yards to go.'

'I know, but it's the only club we have left!'

Fewer people know the story of 'Old Thunder' playing in the Tallahassee Open. American events always have lovely lady markers to send the scores back to the scoring system so that the players get minimum interference on the course.

Thunder Bolt was having a bad day and by the back nine not only had an odd club become airborne, but also the odd four-letter expletive. Tom's language didn't improve over the closing holes and the lady markers were so upset they reported him to the PGA.

Bolt was summoned to the 'PGA caravan' and the Commissioner said, 'These two ladies have turned you in, Tom, for bad language, and I have no alternative but to fine you the statutory $250.'

Bolt scribbled in his cheque book and said, 'Here's $500. Ladies, f… you and f… you.'

On his forty-fifth birthday, Tommy was incensed that an American columnist had written that he was fifty-four.

Collaring the culprit at the course the next day, Tom asked, 'What the hell's the idea?'

'Sorry, Tommy,' replied the journalist, 'it was a typographical error.'

'The hell it was,' snapped Tom. 'It was a perfect 5 and perfect 4.'

Bobby Cole meets the greats

Perhaps the biggest thrill for an amateur golfer would be to win the British Amateur Championship. Contenders do not take this Championship lightly. I remember the young South African, Bobby Cole, having a fierce battle with the wily and feared Frenchman, Henri de Lamaze, at Carnoustie in the semi-finals some years ago.

There was a dispute on the 8th regarding a somewhat dubious drop that Henri felt he was entitled to. Perhaps Henri was serious, perhaps it was gamesmanship. But Cole's Scottish caddie, Tom the Goose, could not see the funny side of de Lamaze's antics. Amid the commotion and bickering

Tom announced in a loud voice to the startled de Lamaze, 'This is golf. Not French comedy.'

Anyway, Cole went on to win and the next day became - at eighteen - one of the youngest Amateur champions ever. With the Championship came an invitation to the prestigious US Masters at Augusta.

The organisers at Augusta give the Amateur Champions from both sides of the Atlantic a really good draw, and on the first day, Bobby found himself paired with Arnold Palmer. He went over to the practice ground and introduced himself to the great man. Palmer, as always, was charming. 'Nice to meet you, Bobby. Let's go out there and enjoy a really good day's golf.'

Bobby had an equally enjoyable second day with Billy Casper, who did nothing but encourage Bobby all the way round. Bobby played nicely and to his credit made the halfway cut.

His third-round partner was the colourful Doug Sanders. As it happened, Sanders was having an orange day - from head to foot; a real crowd pleaser! Bobby walked over to the putting green in front of the revered clubhouse, 'Good morning, Mr Sanders, my name's Bobby Cole and it's a great pleasure for me to be playing with you.'

'Hi,' said Doug, with a smile all over his face. 'Just call me Doug.' 'That's great,' said Bobby. 'Hey,' said Doug, pointing to his stomach, 'I used to have a real big chest, but it just slipped a bit!'

On the final day, Bobby drew the legendary Sam Snead. Just before they were due to be called to the tee, Bobby spotted him on the practice green, Snead, who was never renowned for his bonhomie, was practising his side-saddle putting stroke.

'Good morning, Mr Snead,' said Bobby. 'I'm Bobby Cole and it's a real pleasure to have drawn you today.'

Snead never even looked up from his putting. 'Son,' he said, 'I'll teach you a thing or two out there today,' and continued putting. Bobby froze away to the other end of the green and was beginning to feel quite apprehensive about the round.

They were called to the tee. I should explain that at the Masters the 1st tee is about ten deep and the gallery encircles the whole of this opening par-4 hole. You drive through a valley and over a crest with pine on either side.

'On the tee, Sam Snead,' said the starter. Snead teed his ball, and stepped back as the starter continued, 'Sam Snead, winner of .... Snead touched his hat, addressed the ball and hit a fizzer. The gallery loved it and the applause took a while to die down.

'On the tee, Bobby Cole,' announced the starter. Bobby teed up and

took a pace back so that the starter could embellish on his record . . . but not so much as a word. Not even a 'Bobby Cole, the British Amateur Champion.'

To say Bobby was nervous is probably an understatement. He moved forward and, as he addressed the ball, all he could see were rows and rows of feet and the enormous scoreboard some 45 degrees off on the right. He confessed afterwards that at the time he was wondering whether he would hit the ball at all.

For someone only 10 stone, Cole was a big hitter. He pivoted well, got a clean hit, and when he looked up, much to his relief the ball was soaring down the centre and over the hill.

Snead, of course, in those days was a prodigious hitter. In silence, they moved down the 1st. They progressed over the top of the hill to find Snead's ball a good 40 yards ahead. Snead went to his ball first. Cole then got to his.

Or was it his? He wasn't playing a Wilson!

'Ahem, ahem,' muttered Cole, clearing his throat and trying to catch Sam's attention. 'Mr Snead,' said Bobby, beckoning Snead to the shorter ball. A disgusted Snead and caddie had an embarrassing walk back.

The several-thousand-strong Augusta gallery were loving it. This 10 stone stripling had just out-driven the mighty Snead by 40 yards. Sam clearly was not enjoying it at all. In a loud, severe tone he announced, 'Son, those doggone Wilson golf balls don't go no place.'

Sam Snead and Ben Hogan

It was said that Sam Snead never quite got on with Ben Hogan. I hear Hogan can't play two rounds a day, a marshal once said to Snead.

'How's that?' said Sam.

'Keeps driving into his own divots.'

'If he's that damned good, he'll have to doggone aim six inches to the right.'

Ben Hogan

The first professional tournament at Pinehurst was played in 1940 and won by Ben Hogan.

The architect of Pinehurst Number 2 was one of the great course designers, Donald Ross.

On hearing of Hogan's win, Ross cabled him, 'Excellent, the Greatest.'

Hogan cabled back, 'Undeserving of such praise.'

Ross sent another cable, 'I meant the course.'

Hogan cabled back, 'So did I.'

BACK TO THE ARMCHAIR

Did I ever tell you about the time I got kidnapped? Well, I never thought it would happen to a man of my rugged appearance. They always used to tell me that I looked more like a hit man myself... a hit man for the Ovalteenies.

Anyway, I'd just finished my round at Turnberry and was crossing the road back to the hotel when these two thugs swooped down and bundled me into the back of their car. As we sped off, I must say I was very disappointed to be leaving Turnberry at such a rate of knots. I've always been so impressed with the hotel. I remember they once sacked a waiter for putting his thumb in the soup ... and a topless waitress for two similar offences.

No, no ... I'm digressing again. Where were we? Oh, yes. So these thugs drove for two hours and took me to this deserted old building outside Glasgow, which they'd obviously picked because no one would ever go there ... Celtic Football Ground. No, no ... it wasn't. I must be fair, because Celtic are doing their best to make a go of things. Only last week they signed up two spectators.

I must be honest, though, these two kidnappers had done their homework. They even knew that I used to play a lot of golf with my friend, Maurice. Poor old Maurice. He's sadly no longer with us. I called on him one morning and his wife answered the door.

'I suppose you've come to collect Maurice? I'm afraid he's dead.'

'He isn't!' I exclaimed.

'He's dead.' She repeated over and over again, she was so shocked. I asked her what had happened.

'He went down the garden to cut a cabbage for our Sunday lunch and *bonk* - he was dead.'

'Whatever did you do?' I asked sympathetically.

'Well, I had to open a tin of peas instead,' she replied.

Anyway, the local golf club very kindly agreed to put his ashes in a brass urn and stand the urn in pride of place on the mantlepiece in the club to show their respect for Maurice. However, one or two of the members, not realising the significance of the urn, used to put their cigar and cigarette ash into it.

The other day I heard the Secretary remark, 'My God, he's been dead for six weeks now, but I do believe he's putting on weight.'

BUT ... I'm digressing again ... because these two kidnappers were pretty hard-nosed. They sent a note to the BBC which said, 'How would you like to see Ronnie Corbett strung up on a meat hook?' And the next day they got a letter from the Head of Comedy saying, 'This shows promise, let's have lunch.'

So eventually they issued an ultimatum saying that if the BBC did not leave £5000 in a hollow tree near Glasgow Central Station immediately, I would never be seen again. Eleven months went by, it went through several BBC committees, the ransom note got read out on *Points of View*, and then the kidnappers became fed up with waiting – they let me go, alive and completely unharmed. And the BBC sued them for breach of contract!

MAY I PLAY MULLIGAN?

Strange goings-on in the olive grove

Mark Wilson, that first-class golf correspondent who was with the *Daily Express* for many years, recalls a story about Christy O'Connor. Christy was playing in the World Cup. He had an early morning starting-time the first day and, having had a very long night, was feeling not even a little bright.

Wilson found him in the locker room, his head buried in his strong hands.

'Christy, they're calling you on the tee.'

'Coffee,' replied Christy.

'But you'll be late,' insisted Wilson.

'Black,' groaned Christy.

'Come on, I'll help you.'

'Black and strong,' persisted Christy.

'I'll get it. I'll get it,' said Wilson. 'Just get on the tee.'

'You know the first hole? And the 200-yard marker?' asked Christy. 'You'll find it 200 yards from the tee,' he most helpfully added. 'Well, pace off another 50 yards and wait for me in the olive trees on the left.'

'OK, OK,' said Wilson, shooting off to the restaurant.

Running through the trees balancing his cup of black coffee, Wilson reached the appointed spot. Three balls had already arrived on the fairway as the starter announced, 'And also representing Ireland, Christy O'Connor.' The applause was silenced – the gallery could not believe that O'Connor himself was clattering about in the olive grove some 50 yards off line. The ball almost holed out in Wilson's coffee cup. Perhaps one of the greatest nominated shots of all time.

A few quick slurps of coffee later, Christy's ball reappeared from the grove. A plucky pitch and putt secured a par and O'Connor went on to shoot a most commendable 4-under-par 68.

Talking to him afterwards, our intrepid correspondent asked, 'Christy, how come you've just gone round in 68 when you're pissed?'

'It's quite simple,' said Christy, 'because I practise when I'm pissed.'

Rained off

One of golf's finest writers, Peter Dobereiner, was doing a column during the European Open at Walton Heath on wet-weather golf.

It was pouring with rain – the perfect day for gathering first-hand information. Soon, Peter spotted Tom Weiskopf half drowned and about to finish his round.

What better man could he ask? An articulate American whose golf record spoke for itself. Perhaps he would offer tips to the club golfer on the subject. Perhaps some of the inner professional secrets of wet-weather play would be revealed. Peter pushed the microphone towards Tom's lips in eager anticipation.

'Playing golf in the rain,' said Tom, giving the question his full consideration, 'is a pain in the ass!'

Flaming cheek

Peter Thomson, the great Australian golfer who has done so well on the US Seniors Tour, has a good sense of humour, but talking to him is a little like crossing a cow field. If you don't keep your wits about you, you put your foot right in it.

Some years ago, he showed me a letter he had received from a fan. Not all golfing fans are great spellers, as you'll see.

The letter read, 'Dear Mr Thomson, I always follow you when I get to the golf tournaments and my wife is a tremendous fan. Could you please send me a singed photograph of yourself ...'

Thommo borrowed a photograph of himself from the Press Tent and with a match carefully burned the edges. He sent the gentleman a singed photograph. Surprise, surprise. A week later another letter from the same address appeared:

'Dear Mr Thomson, Thank you very much indeed for the photograph but I would appreciate if you could send me another as this one has been signed all round the edges.'

Slanderous allegations

Lee Trevino was playing in a pro-am at a golf complex in Australia. At the clubhouse that day, he had joked, 'The room I have at my hotel is so small that the rats are all round-shouldered.'

The hotel manager was understandably very upset at this remark and asked for a public apology from Lee at the presentation dinner that night.

Lee was happy to oblige. His speech that evening contained the following handsome retraction: 'I apologise if I upset anybody today when I said that the rats in this hotel are round-shouldered. They're not!'

The
HALFWAY
HUT

Quote
Tommy Bolt, after being fined for breaking wind on the 1st tee: 'You guys are trying to take all the colour out of the game?'

CADDIES

One Tooth Jock

Ben Wright, the British commentator with CBS, tells this marvellous story of the day, many years ago, when 'One Tooth Jock' was assigned to caddie for him in the Bowmaker Tournament at Sunningdale.

Ben had never seen One Tooth Jock before. But as the caddie master made his way to the line of caddies, Ben was left in no doubt as to who was carrying his bag! Jock's Bugs Bunny grin said it all.

'I'll meet you in five minutes on the practice ground,' said Ben.

Ben was there five minutes later. One Tooth Jock had gone for a quick snort of local brew to top up the level from the previous night's festivities, but eventually he arrived — even if slightly inebriated!

The practice over, Ben — who was playing with the great Bobby Locke — went for lunch and instructed Jock to meet him on the 1st tee.

While Wright tucked into a good lunch of roast beef and Yorkshire pudding, One Tooth Jock was tucking into a large bottle of Beefeaters best, somewhere out on the other course. When Wright got to the 1st tee, there was no Jock and no clubs, with the result that he had to borrow a set — a most unsatisfactory state of affairs.

Ben, a single-figure player, coped well. He and Locke were several under par when they came over the hill at the 7th to find One Tooth Jock weaving across the fairway with Ben's disarrayed set on his back.

'Before you con- conde- condemn me,' spluttered Jock. 'I think you should know that I've been out here on the course all the time. But I was with the wrong match. I thought, this is odd, I've been with the match for six holes and no one has asked me for a club yet.'

The water of life

Doug Sanders once arrived at the Open with a streaming cold. The raw Scottish weather wasn't doing much to improve it. But Doug had his small silver hip-flask with him. It was filled with the 'good stuff'.

The flamboyant Doug was dressed from head to foot in a delicate shade of lilac that day. He was on a two-week trip and had brought twenty-one pairs of shoes with him!

The weather was grey and cold and, not wishing to be seen drinking on the course, Doug skilfully hid his flask under an orange-and-white striped towel. On the pretext of giving his nose a prolonged wipe, he was, in fact, having a good gulp of Johnny Walker's best!

Halfway though the practice round, it started to pour down. The course became sodden.

'Isn't there a dry place on this course?' asked Doug.

His old Scottish caddie, who had hardly said anything all day, piped up, 'You could try the back of my throat, sir.'

In Thomson's footsteps

The story goes that Doug Sanders arrived one year in Melbourne to play in the Australian Open. Melbourne has some of the prettiest golf courses to be found anywhere, and all the best ones are on a thirty-mile-long sand belt (as in the Surrey and Berkshire area, where beautiful courses like Wentworth, Sunningdale and Berkshire are to be found).

Doug had a bit of luck. He was given a very good caddie. In fact, this particular man had always caddied for Peter Thomson on that course.

Off they went down the first and arrived at Sanders' drive. The hole was 428 yards.

'What club is it?' he asked.

'Mr Thomson always hits a 6-iron from here,' said the caddie.

'That looks about right,' said Doug, as the caddie handed him the 6-iron. He hit a good solid 6 and the ball finished in the centre of the green.

The next hole was 155 yards par-3, off a slightly elevated tee. 'Mr Thomson usually hits a 7-iron here,' said the caddie.

'Right,' said Doug, 'give me the 7-iron.' Another beauty landed in the centre of the green.

The 3rd was a short par-4, dog-legging round some trees. Doug went the longer route off the tee and was on the left edge of the fairway. From this side, it opened up the green.

'What does Peter play from here?'

'Mr Thomson nearly always hits a 9-iron from here,' came the reply. A good 9-iron was struck and it finished some 7 feet past the pin.

The 4th is a longish par-4 with a blind second to a green that is placed over a brow and sits in a dish. Doug's drive was in the perfect spot that the caddie had nominated, on the right half of the fairway.

'Now,' said Doug, 'what club does Mr Thomson hit here?'

'Mr Thomson always hits a 4-iron from here, straight over that marker post.'

Sanders hit the 4-iron as requested. To his surprise, when they got over the brow, his ball was 20 yards short of the green.

'I thought you said Mr Thomson always hits a 4-iron from there,' said a puzzled Doug.

'He does,' replied the caddie, 'and it's a funny thing, but he always finishes 20 yards short, too.'

Well travelled

Neil Armstrong, the US astronaut, was playing in the pro-celebrity series at Gleneagles. His caddie was one of the touring variety who had caddied in Spain, Portugal, Morocco and several other countries.

On the way to the 1st tee, Armstrong was questioning the caddie politely about the many different countries he had visited.

'But, Mr Armstrong,' interrupted the caddie, 'you've walked on the moon and you want to hear about the travellings of a caddie?'

'Oh, yes, please,' replied Armstrong. 'The moon is the only place I've ever been to.'

Unidentified flying object

Harry Weetman had enormous hands and shoulders and was probably the longest hitter of his era. His was certainly not a pretty swing, more one of blood and thunder. In fact, when he belted one off a tight lie on the fairway, it is no exaggeration to say you could feel the ground shake.

Dear old Harry was certainly rugged. One day at the Gleneagles foursomes he was firing balls down the practice ground in dense fog. As he whacked away with his 2-iron a sickening shriek came from the far end of the strip. Clearly a caddie had caught one of Harry's best full tosses.

Full of sympathy, Harry yelled down the practice ground at the top of his voice, 'What's the matter with you, you baby? It's only a bit of rubber.'

Harry was a great gladiator rather than the product of finishing school.

Quote
Ben Hogan was probably the golfer nearest to perfection. He once said:
'I had a dream last night. I dreamt I had seventeen 1s and a 2. And when I woke up, gee... I was mad.'

COOK IN THE SOUP

Disaster at La Manga

John H. Cook is not necessarily a household name. Those keener followers of golf will remember he used to play the circuit in the early 1970s. The circuit was a little different in those days.

John Cook turned up at La Manga, having not had a particularly good run in the preceding Continental events. It was the Spanish Open that week. John had to pre-qualify. This is never an enviable task and John felt that part of his lack of success was due to not having a good caddie. Local caddies in Europe are a bit hit-and-miss — mainly miss.

John walked down to the caddies' area where there were seemingly a hundred or so caddies and the caddie master spoke decent English. This was his chance. Slipping 500 pesetas into the caddie master's palm, John said, 'I want a good caddie who can speak English.'

Slipping the 500 pesetas back into John's palm, the caddie master replied, 'Speaka da English? Dis lot don't even speaka da Spanish.' The tone of yet another week of disappointment seemed set. Or was it?

John, in spite of his twelve-year-old caddie who had been nothing but a nuisance, came to the last hole 1-under-par. This, and perhaps even par, would make it. The last hole on La Manga's North Course is a par-4. John was on the front of this very long and sloping green in two. Now, could he get down in two more to clinch it! The young caddie was sent to attend the pin. Because of John's good sign language and an odd tweak of the ear, he actually seemed to be alive to what was going on and his excitement had run to a few 'Buenos'.

Cookie's 20-yard putt across a left/right slope was not an easy one. There was a 6-foot break on it and the last third of it was downhill. As the ball ran towards the hole, Cookie's caddie could no longer contain himself and was jumping up and down. The ball was going straight for the hole. For a ghastly moment, Cookie thought the caddie was going to leave the pin in.

'Take it out. Take it out,' yelled Cookie, but the ball came up 9 inches short.

It's hard to say whether it was the sheer excitement of misinterpretation but the small lad was so impressed with Cookie's putt that he gave him the rest, kicking the ball back to Cookie as though it were a practice round!

Poor Cookie's 71, plus two penalty strokes, turned into a 73 and, as they say in the trade, 'Cookie was down the road again.' He'd missed by one single shot.

Silent partner

Following the Spanish escapade, Cookie had shown little form. He confessed to playing so badly that he had received a Get Well card from the Inland Revenue. Although he'd made the odd cut, he had frequently been frustrated by just missing it.

After 34 holes of the Open at Royal Birkdale, it was looking like a sure-fire cut-making position — until the inevitable brace of sixes turned up and Cookie missed the cut by one. It was a very dejected John Cook who was changing his shoes in the locker-room. A big chance had just slipped through his fingers.

Cookie was therefore quite surprised when his luck seemed to change. A gentleman approached him and asked if he'd missed the cut. Cookie said he had, and the gentleman asked whether, as they were short of pros in the King's Tournament in Morocco, John would like to take part. It was a great deal: all expenses paid, £500 as well as what he could win. At last, thought John, my luck must be changing. It was. It was about to get worse.

King Hussan's pro-am was a very splendid affair. Over a thousand guests had been flown in. The event was held on the King's own golf course in the palace grounds at Skirat. What a weekend it threatened to be.

John teed off at 8.10 the following morning. It was a lovely hot day and he had three most amicable partners. One of them, in fact, was the King's own military man, General Medbou.

The General made some amusing remarks, but was not a very talented golfer. In spite of Cookie helping him with his game, giving him yardages and reading the greens, he never came in.

'What a good day,' chuckled John, as he was changing his shoes in the luxurious locker-room. Cookie's luck, though, was short-lived. A 2-inch mortar shell wiped out half of the adjacent wall and smashed its way through a window. Troops rushed in brandishing machine guns and poor old Cookie was taken prisoner!

Out on the palace lawn, he joined many other guests who were lying face down on the grass and being guarded by soldiers. There were sounds of explosions and gunfire. Cookie, and this could only happen to Cookie, had landed himself right in the middle of a military coup!

After an hour or so face down on the ground, John's arm was tiring and he let it fall to his side. A soldier gave it a good whack with the butt of his rifle. Another half hour went by and two helicopters zoomed over the lawn.

Chaos ensued and, amid the fighting, most of the guests rushed to the palace entrance. Cookie was not last in the line and, making his way down several long corridors, he found his way into a kitchen and dived into a large cooking cauldron.

Eventually, he was taken prisoner again and returned to the palace lawn. One of the Spanish pros had still been on the course when the coup started. The poor chap got chased by a small platoon of soldiers who were taking pot-shots at him. The Spaniard proved to be a fast runner and, when he reached the sea shore, a very nifty swimmer! As the bullets were zipping round his head, he swam out to sea and finally managed to get to the safety of dry land further down the coast.

Meanwhile, back at the palace, the loyalist troops had regained power and all the rebels had been captured.

Said Cookie, 'The one thing that really upset me was that it turned out that my pro-am partner, General Medbou, was the leader of the coup. I clubbed him and gave him the line on every green. You'd have thought he would have told me to go and hide in a bunker for a couple of hours!'

Quote
Peter Alliss commentating live on a streaker leaping across the 18th green at an Open Championship: 'I don't know why such a little thing is causing all this fuss.'

The last straw

ou would have thought that Cookie would still be shaking a week later. He was.

He arrived at the German Open having missed the French. He had a good practice round and was greatly encouraged. The German Open was at Bremen, a most attractive pine-tree-lined course where the gaps between the trees were not over-generous.

Neil Coles, who was one of the best drivers on the tour, looked to be favourite, along with Peter Thomson. Cookie, by this time in good spirits, arrived at the course some three-quarters of an hour before his tee-off time. To his horror, he discovered that some cad had stolen his golf shoes, the only pair he had at the club. After a great deal of unsuccessful searching, he had to borrow a pair, which hurt so badly after nine holes that he had to discard them and play barefoot. He scored 34 for the first nine and 44 for the second. Another cut-missing week was on the way.

Cookie was determined to get it right. He'd already entered for the Swiss Open. This event is played at that beautiful ski and golf resort, Crans-sur-Sierre, some 100 miles east of Geneva. At 5000 feet the course is nearly as high as the prices. Going to Crans with £200 in your pocket is about as effective as trying to scale Everest in plimsolls!

Cookie had arrived in plenty of time. He wanted to work on his game — he wanted to clean the course. For a start, playing golf at 5000 feet is a novel experience. Because of the thinness of the air, the ball flies faster and further. A pro who-hits a 9-iron 130 yards on the fly will suddenly find that at 5000 feet it goes about 150 yards. That makes a difference of about a club and a half.

The driver also goes a great deal further and 300 yards plus for a pro is 'ordinaire' rather than raw talent. Therefore, it's everyday stuff for the longer hitters to be reaching holes of 500 yards with as little as a drive and 7-iron.

Over several rounds, Cookie sussed out the course. If you are going to hit the ball much further you must be more accurate off the tee. You soon run out of fairway and certain holes become very narrow, particularly the 6th. It's a short par-4 — almost driveable. You play through an avenue of fir trees which ungenerously narrow about 200 yards from the tee. A 5-iron from the tee, coupled with a wedge to the green, is the secret to this hole. I once remember the great Roberto de Vicenzo, one of the straightest drivers in the world, falling foul of it. A drive only yards off line penetrated the pines. Everyone heard the hollow echo. No one ever found the ball. When you've lost one, it's easy to reload with the driver again and lose two. He did, and having led the tournament to that point, a 4-iron, a half wedge and a putt eventually earned him a 7.

Sometimes, when playing a course, it's better not to know the fate that has befallen others. But Cookie had done his research, even to finding out how Peter Townsend had once carded a course record of 61 — surely one of the most deserving course records in history — only to last half an hour. The Italian Baldo Dassu marched in with a 60 right on top of him!

Inspired by this, Cookie woke up early on the morning of the first round. He had a good mid-morning starting time. And a stiff neck! Of course, his local hotelier knew just the man to fix it. He would have stood a better chance if Jim had fixed it! One good wrench and Cookie was reduced from a potential three-quarter swing to something that Doug Sanders would call a three-quarter swing.

Cookie battled on gamely, but he was virtually chipping the ball around the course. Under the circumstances, his 84 might have been a worthy effort. He improved to an 82 the second day, but his thoughts were now on getting his neck better and back to Birmingham to pre-qualify for the Birmingham Classic.

It's a long drive from Crans to Birmingham, but it was done in two days and the neck was better. Cookie had a good night's sleep and was feeling in top form as he drove into the Copt Heath car park. Hopping out of his car, he spotted David Jones. 'What time are you off, John?' asked Jones.

'10.20'

'10.20?'

'Yes, 10.20.'

'Are you sure?' said Jones. 'I know we're not playing together. You must be on the Coventry course.'

It was the first time ever in Britain that two courses had been used for pre-qualifying in a PGA event. Cookie checked with the starter and, sure enough, he was pre-qualifying at Coventry. A stunned Cookie got back in

his car. He was teeing off in forty minutes and it is a good half hour's drive to Coventry.

Pulling out all the stops, he roared into the car park as the starter was calling him to come to the tee. He jumped into his spikes, grabbed his bag and made it with nothing to spare.

Needless to say, his opening shot did not quite come from the sweet spot. But it finished in play. In fact, the adrenalin was flowing sufficiently so that he hit the turn in 34. I should explain that Cookie had never played the course before and had no caddie. The 12th is a blind tee-shot over a brow. Cookie hit a cracker on what he thought to be a good line over the marker post. The marker post was not for the Championship tee, though. There is a very large tree that encroaches on the right of the fairway. Cookie's ball gave it a jolly good clatter before changing course and diving into the adjacent river. A drop out into the rough for a penalty shot and a horrid 6 went on the card. His 72 missed the pre-qualifying.

Mr Cook subsequently chose to earn his living by the safer method of running a pub. It was called 'The Nine Black Cats'.

Quote
'I'm so broke', complained one caddie to another, 'the bottom is falling out of my trousers.'
'You're lucky,' said the other. 'My bottom is falling through someone else's trousers.'

HOW'S IT LYING, CLIVE?

My friend and co-author Clive Clark needs little introduction to BBC golf viewers. Ever since Seve Ballesteros visited two bus shelters and nine car parks during his final and victorious round in the 1979 Open Championship at Lytham, Clive has found his feet permanently planted on the ground as opposed to the commentary box. It always surprises me that he manages to get in so many places at once and that even when he's buried in 8 feet of rough, Peter Alliss always seems able to find him.

Clive is no mean golfer and apart from winning several PGA Tour events he represented Great Britain in both Walker and Ryder Cup teams. He also finished third in the 1967 Open Championship at Hoylake behind Jack Nicklaus and Roberto de Vicenzo.

This chapter is devoted to some of Clive's stories about the horrors of a commentator's life and about his own golfing days or, as they say every Sunday when I'm in waist-deep rough, 'How's it lying, Clive?'

The filler's art

Spare a thought for the poor commentator when a tournament is going through a flat patch, desperately finding something to talk about — to 'fill' until things liven up. Here's Clive's frank exposé of the filler's art and a tribute to the evergreen Harry Carpenter.

One of the longest 'fills' Clive ever had to do on televised golf was at the 1979 Walker Cup matches at Muirfield. They had cameras placed from the 12th hole in.

On the opening morning, the first foursome should have reached the 12th by 10.50 a.m., the time they went on the air. Unfortunately, the golf was so slow that come 10.45 they were only halfway down the 9th!

Ricky Tilling, the Director, said to Harry Carpenter, 'We are going to need a prolonged introduction, Harry, and then talk to Clive until we've got some pictures.'

Harry is brilliant at filling and has the rare ability to time himself to the second. After his 'prolonged' introduction, he continued, '... And one of our commentators, Clive Clark, is with me. Clive, you've played both Walker and Ryder Cup golf. What sort of additional pressures do you have to deal with when you're representing your country?'

Harry is an expert at keeping the questions rolling and all went well until question five, 'And who on the American team has particularly impressed you?'

'Well ...' Clive said, knowing he had a complete blank. He couldn't think of a single American name. It's during that split second that you see your BBC contract dissolving before your eyes.

'... I was out on the practice ground yesterday ...' Clive continued, waffling as best he knew how and praying for inspiration, '... and ... and there was this young player, Clarke ... Doug Clarke, the youngest member of their team, and though he's only nineteen, he's a most accomplished player and the fact that he hits the ball low is undoubtedly going to help him play this particular course.' Clive was out — home and dry. The panic was over. Imagine having the good luck to have your namesake playing on their team!

At least, he *thought* he was out and home and dry, until Harry's next question, 'And who else on the American team impressed you?'

Clive looked up at Harry, who is not altogether a tall man. 'Oh no,' he thought, 'Harry, you don't know what you're doing to me!' Fortunately, he's a little taller than Harry and he could just see the first name on the scoreboard over the top of his head.

'Well,' Clive said, feeling that he had just recovered from being six down with six to play, 'there is Jay Sigel, the most experienced and probably the steadiest player on their team...'

You don't need too many moments like that in front of camera!

Quote
Sign at the British Open at Royal St George's in a hospitality marquee close to the 4th green: 'The golfers are trying to putt quietly while you drink! PLEASE RECIPROCATE.'

Quick change

Clive has some wild stories to tell about starters and their ways. The worst thing that can happen to a starter, says Clive, is for him to get your name wrong. He not only shows to the gallery that he doesn't know what he's talking about, but he also stands a very good chance of getting a wedge between the ears.

One day, Clive was about to tee off at the Glen Campbell Los Angeles Open. The starter there either suffered from severe myopia, had had too many the night before, or had a typist of dubious talent.

Somehow the C in Clive got joined up and poor Clive was announced as, 'And next on the tee from London, England, we have Olive Clark.'

That's a hard one to live down! You can see why Clive bears a bit of a grudge against starters.

Mum's the word

But that's not all. Another starter put his foot in it at a Variety Club Pro-Am outside London.

Clive arrived on the tee and the starter introduced him and his partners. Clive teed off first, followed by his 10-handicap partner. They both hit good ones. The 12-handicap partner went and, though he connected quite well, his ball just missed the fairway.

The last of the four was a 20-handicapper. From the number of quick waggles he made at the ball, he was obviously very nervous. At last he got the club back. The gallery must have been wondering if it was ever going to happen. He took a quick flash at the ball which popped up into the sun and disappeared over some nearby tennis courts.

The luckless fellow went to his caddie to reload. Meanwhile, one of the spectators, a lady, had assumed the ball had gone down the middle and was walking down the fairway.

The starter yelled a blurting 'fore' and then, turning to Clive and shaking his head, muttered angrily, 'Who is that silly old bag?'

Embarrassment almost prevented Clive from admitting that it was, in fact, none other than Mrs Clark ... Clive's mother.

Red braces – red faces

This is Clive's favourite starter story of all time. The setting is the Australian PGA event some years ago. The field was sent on its way by a starter who stood on the 1st tee in an open-neck shirt and rather baggy pants which remained waist-high due only to the tenacity of a pair of bright red braces. The starter zealously held on to the microphone like a kid holds on to a box of chocolates. Bet you've got one in your club — he always volunteers to do the auction!

Clive's playing partners that day were Peter Thomson and Gay Brewer. First away was Brewer.

'On the tee,' announced the starter, 'we have, from the United States of America, Gay Brewer, winner of the Alcan Tournament, the US Masters, the Pacific Masters, the Greater Greensboro Open and countless other tournaments. Ladies and Gentlemen, I give you Gay Brewer.' Brewer hit a beauty.

'Next on the tee,' continued the starter, 'we have your very own favourite, Peter Thomson . . .' the gallery applauded again, but they were shouted down, '. . . twice winner of the New Zealand Open, five times winner of the Australian Open—' Thomson couldn't stand it any longer and smashed one down the centre while Red Braces was still at full throttle.

Now it was Clive's turn. 'On the tee, Clive Clark.' Clive waited for a further announcement. Nothing happened. Not very charitable considering he had won two tournaments that year and had been third in the British Open. He addressed the ball and was just getting comfortable when Red Braces started again. 'Clark in 1967 tied for fifth place in the South African Pepsi Cola Tournament.'

The next day Clive arrived at the tee in time to hear the announcement of the first player of the threeball in front. 'From Nationalist China, we have Cho Ling-low. He doesn't swing the scales far, but my word, would you watch him hit this one.' Just imagine how Mr Cho was feeling. All of 5-feet nothing, he had just been proclaimed as one of the all-time long hitters.

He wound himself up like a corkscrew and attempted to give the ball an almighty whack. The result was his drive bounced three times before it dribbled into the 200-yard cross bunkers.

It was at this stage that Clive decided he couldn't stand the antics of Red Braces any longer. He went over to him and had a few words, explaining that the day before he had been very disappointed when no

mention had been made of his finest achievement in golf. 'I'm very sorry,' Red Braces said. 'What was it?' Clive told him.

Again, it was Brewer's honour and again Red Braces went through the entire ritual. Thomson looked extremely bored, and when it came to his turn, he snubbed the man for a second time by hitting off before the announcement was over.

Now it was Clive's turn. 'Next on the tee, from London, England, we have Clive Clark who, in 1967, tied for fifth place in the South African Pepsi Cola Tournament. But his proudest moment surely came when he won the Glastonbury Sweetbreads.'

The gallery burst into laughter. If Clive had known Red Braces was going to swallow that one, he'd have told him he'd won the Grand National as well!

The sharp end

'Cutty', as he was known, was not a bad golfer. Henry Cotton himself thought he would have reached scratch had it not been for his weak hands. Cutty cut the ball, and he also had difficulty getting out of rough.

Having an inkling about club design, Cutty decided the only thing for it was to design a special club for rough. One night he went to his workshop and ground the leading edge of his sand-iron down to a razor sharp edge.

The next day he was playing at Sunningdale. The first moment to try the club occurred at the 17th during a tense moment in the Sunday four-ball. The ball was buried in heather.

Cutty gave it his all. There was a large whoosh as dust, dirt, rough and heather exploded in all directions.

Heads turned skywards. But after ten seconds, it was clear that no golf ball was up there. Strange, they thought, as they inspected the huge trench looking for clues.

Excitedly, one of Cutty's opponents yelled, 'It's there, it's there!' All the heads peered down the fairway again.

'No, not there. THERE.'

He pointed to the ball, which was firmly impaled on the head of Cutty's new sand-iron.

FLUFFS, BUMBLES AND SHANKS

Not 'another' speech

I think it is fair to say that not many people enjoy having to make a speech. Even fewer people enjoy having to stand up at the Grosvenor House in the Great Room in front of 1000 guests!

I remember Donald Steel, the well-read correspondent of the *Sunday Telegraph*, once making an excellent speech in that very room, at the PGA dinner some years ago. It was in the days when that stalwart of professional golf, Major Bywaters, was the Secretary. Donald, an excellent speaker, romanced about the PGA. He did, however, find it strange that the Professional Golfers' headquarters was at the Oval cricket ground. He had observed during his occasional visits to the Oval that Bywaters had on his desk an 'in' tray and an 'out' tray for letters. He also noticed that there was a third tray with the letters LBW stamped on it. It was only on that very evening that he had worked out for himself that in fact there was no link with cricket whatsoever. 'It did not,' he said, 'stand for leg before wicket, but rather, let the buggers wait.'

I also remember one very nervous captain of the R & A speaking. It was clear from the start that he was not relishing his duty. He timidly

advanced. 'I would much rather play golf in front of you than speak. Even at sixty years of age I still manage to boast a 4 handicap, whereas at speaking I'm closer to 20. ...'

He was interrupted at this point by a wag from one of the near tables, who cried out 'Sit down, you've just been pushed to 24.' I suppose the task ahead of him was similar to trying to hole a slippery 4-footer for a 6 when your opponent's caddie has just trodden on your line.

A further moment of speech-making embarrassment comes to mind involving Harry Weetman, who was Ryder Cup Captain when the tournament was at Royal Birkdale in 1965. Early in the week, Harry and his team had a dinner given for them by one of the leading golf clubs in the area. The Captain of the club, an old Harrovian, spoke beautifully for ten minutes. Then it was Harry's turn to reply. 'Mr President, Mr Captain and members of ...' Harry broke off. Never a man to mince words, he continued looking towards the Captain, '... what do they call the club?'

The pro from Milwaukee

The image of Walter Deneki still lingers on in the sand hills at Hillside. It was in 1965 when Walt confidently strode on to the 1st tee to commence his qualifying round in the Open Championship. A broad-shouldered man in his mid-thirties and tidily dressed, he looked every inch a pro.

However, it became evident when he made a swing that this was not the case. Further confirmation came when he handed in his card. His score was 112.

When questioned by the R & A, Walter broke down and confessed. He was in fact a postman from Milwaukee and not a 'professional' as he had stated on his entry form.

'It was visions of getting my hands on that crock of gold that made me do it. I wanted to see my name on the cup alongside Arnold Palmer.'

Confident that Deneki would now waste no time in returning to the States, the R & A nominated a substitute for the second day's play. But no such luck. Deneki was there for his official starting time of 11.03. After all, the ball hadn't run for him yesterday. He was determined to show the world he could play the game in the highest company.

After two out of bounds on the 1st, and an 8 on the 2nd he was in trouble. Only courage and perseverence produced a score of 116. His total of 228 narrowly missed the cut by 88 shots.

Many people would understandably have been discouraged by these efforts, but not our Walt. He was eager to share his new experiences with the rest of the golfing world and announced to the press, 'I want to say that your English size ball is perfect for these conditions. If I'd been using the big ball, I'd have been in all sorts of trouble!'

A journalist's lot

'Michael Attenborough, international golfer and London publisher . . .' dictated Mark Wilson of the *Express* to his copytaker in Fleet Street.

Several amateur events went by and Wilson became aware that Attenborough seemed to be giving him the cold shoulder.

At the English Amateur, Wilson spoke up for himself, 'Have I done anything to offend you?'

Attenborough, an amiable man at heart, dived into his hip pocket and produced the piece from Wilson that had been lying heavily in his wallet for some weeks. It read, 'Michael Attenborough, international golfer and London publican . . .'

As Mark will tell you, a golf journalist's life is never an easy one. He is heavily involved in the annual PGA Tour book. At the end of the year, the players vote on 'best long iron player', 'best driver', 'best putter', etc.. The winner of each section then contributes a section on 'how to do it'.

The award to the 'best bunker player' went to Irishman Eamonn Darcy. Bunker play being a fascinating subject, Wilson had reserved in excess of six pages. After some weeks, he caught up with Darcy. Wilson's pen was poised, his notebook at the ready to capture the torrents of vital information that were about to leave Darcy's lips.

'You open the face,' said Eamonn.

'Yes, yes,' said Wilson.

'And you give it a bash.'

Arthur the great

Arthur Lees hailed from Sheffield, was Sunningdale Professional for twenty-seven years and came back from the dead when he fought off cancer fourteen years ago. At seventy-eight, if he doesn't play eighteen holes, he plays thirty-six. He has retained his Yorkshire accent, calls a spade a spade, and is as tenacious as any terrier that ever came from Freddie Trueman's home county. Never short of an opinion and always willing to give it, he is to golf what Al Reid was to the Light Programme.

Some weeks after a second operation for cancer, Arthur appeared back at Sunningdale.

He looked frail, but his strength was rapidly growing. One of his first games was with David Wickins, that kindly extrovert and Chairman of British Car Auctions. Wickins was returning to the clubhouse to write Arthur a three-figure cheque, when he was stopped by a Member.

'How is Arthur playing?' he asked.

'How is Arthur playing?' snapped Wickins. 'What's left of him just went round in 67!'

Arthur was a great gambler. In his first Ryder Cup match in 1947 at Portland, Oregon, he stood on the 1st tee and said to his opponent, Ed 'Porky' Oliver, 'What do you want to play for, then?'

'$100,' replied Oliver.

'Don't make me laugh,' said Lees indignantly, 'I've come out here for a proper game.'

In all, Arthur represented Britain in four Ryder Cup matches and won such tournaments as the Irish Open and Dunlop Masters. Like Norman von Nida, he is a most generous man. There are so many stories about Arthur, many about his gambling deeds, that it is difficult to know where to start.

A few years ago, Gary Player's son Wayne came to stay in Sunningdale. Wayne was about eighteen and a pretty confident scratch player. He was out, in true Player style, practising his bunker shots at 8 o'clock one morning. At about 10.30 he was still practising from the same bunker when Arthur came past. Young Wayne's bunker play was quite exemplary. A blanket would have covered practically all of the fifty or so balls on the green. 'I'll just tell you where you're going wrong,' said Arthur.

Slightly taken aback, Wayne could not resist telling him, 'My Dad is Gary Player and he taught me how to play these shots.'

'Ah!' exclaimed Arthur. 'And I taught your Dad!'

As you may have gathered, the slightest hint to Arthur that someone might beat him is like a red rag to a bull. One morning some years ago, Arthur came into his shop. His assistants were reading *Golf Illustrated* as it was then.

'Mr Lees,' said one, 'have you seen there is a chap in here called Trevellion who claims to be the best putter in the world? He says he will challenge anyone for £1000.'

'Is that so?' said Arthur indignantly. 'Get him on the phone.'

Mr Trevellion, who in fact was a cartoonist and had invented a style of putting with the right hand way down the bottom of the shaft, somehow

managed to play off 24, in spite of being 'the best putter in the world'! Arthur's assistant eventually raised him.

'Is that Paul Trevellion?' snorted Arthur. 'Now, I understand you'll putt anyone for £1000.'

'That's correct,' said Trevellion.

'Right, then,' said Arthur, 'we'll do some putting from 30 feet, then 20 feet, then 10 feet—'

At this point, Arthur was interrupted by Trevellion, 'Oh no, Mr Lees, I only putt for £1000 from 4 feet on the 16th green at Enfield.'

'Four feet, 4 feet?' scoffed Arthur. 'They give me those!'

Back in the early 1950s, a gentleman called Major Henderson appeared in Surrey. The Major was a good golfer and held a handicap of scratch. Arthur was sometimes slow to recognise the skills of others and one day in the bar when someone said to him, 'That Major Henderson is a good player,' Arthur swiftly replied, 'A good player? A good player? Never heard of him.'

'Oh yes,' insisted the observer. 'Give him a shot or two, Arthur, and he'll give you a good game.'

'Good game? Good game? I'll paralyse him,' snapped Arthur. 'He can have 4 up start and I'll play him for anything he likes.'

Well, apparently it was like a clay pigeon shoot — they were all having a pot at Arthur. 'I'll have £25, Arthur,' said one. 'Make mine £50,' said another. 'I'll have £100 on Henderson, Arthur.' And before you could say 'Jack Robinson', Arthur had got £1100 against him.

The date was fixed. They were to play the Old at Sunningdale. I remember Arthur recounting the tale many years later in the bar in front of an intent audience. 'Must have been quite a match,' said one.

'Quite a match? I'll just say it was. That Major Henderson had been practising a lot, like. Do you know he reached the turn in 33 and I was giving him 4 up start?'

'Oh, no.'

'Shame.'

'What bad luck, Arthur' ... came a chorus from the bar.

'How many down were you, Arthur?' asked a past Captain.

'Down?' snapped Arthur, 'Down? I was paralysing him. I was 3 up. Out in 27, then I went 3, 3, 4, 2. Thank you — thank you very much — 6 and 5. And do you know,' said Arthur, his feathers clearly ruffled, 'he wouldn't have a bye.'

I am the greatest

It was some years ago when Paul Trevellion acclaimed himself to be 'the greatest putter in the world'. To add substance to this claim, he had challenged the likes of Nicklaus and Palmer to a contest for vast sums. Needless to say, both declined. With the exception of Arthur Lees, there also seemed to be a singular lack of interest from any British pro in putting on the 16th green at Enfield from only 4 feet!

Ian Wooldridge, feature writer and broadcaster, caught wind of this and felt there was a good story. After a phone call, all was arranged. Wooldridge was to meet 'the greatest putter in the world' at his home in Enfield.

Arriving at Trevellion's home, Wooldridge was greeted by Trevellion who was togged up in his Arnold Palmer visor, Jack Nicklaus shirt, Gary Player slacks and plimsolls.

They then ventured across the dual carriageway which separated Paul's semi from the local golf club. Trevellion led the way through a hedge and held apart the barbed wire fence, motioning Wooldridge to crawl through.

'Slight problem here, old chap,' said Wooldridge. 'We've got three outside broadcast vans. Can't we go in through the front door?'

'Then we certainly have a problem,' said Trevellion. 'I'm not a member.'

A delicate situation was resolved by Wooldridge calling the Secretary. He explained that 'the best putter in the world' lived only across the dual carriageway and it would be a great shame if the viewers were deprived of seeing him in action.

The Secretary eventually agreed and it was decided that Trevellion would play out to the appointed green. What better plan could there be for the documentary. The viewers would then have a chance to examine the long game of 'the best putter in the world'.

Four air shots and Trevellion was still on the tee. It was a slow journey to the 16th green. By the time they got there, the weather had intervened — it was pouring with rain. There was no filming and the question, 'Was Paul Trevellion the best putter in the world?' remains unanswered.

SOME GEMS FROM THE SUGGESTIONS BOOKS

Secretaries view it with distain. Members vent their wrath through it. Committees pull their hair out trying to think of smart replies. What is it? The Club Suggestion Book.

This fascinating book is to be found in most clubhouses and in some cases may even date back to the turn of the century. In this chapter we look at some of the most humorous and interesting comments from a selection of the top clubs in the south of England. We are most grateful to the clubs concerned for their co-operation in providing the material.

Suggestion: (1902) That a Whisky and Schweppes/Whisky and Perrier be 10d and not 1/2d.

Reply: The price will be reduced to 1/-.

Suggestion: (1909) That 3/6 for a small bottle (4 glasses) of very inferior Port, undecanted and muddy, is very high and useless. Excellent Port can be sold at 6d a glass.
Reply: This shall be rectified immediately.

Suggestion: (1913) That a man be put in charge of the car shed to see that cars are not interfered with, and also to put down sawdust on oil dripping on the floor. All pressure tyres are damaged by standing in pools of oil.

Last Saturday, my car was removed from the car shed to make room for another, and left standing outside. The idiot who did it, evidently tried to move the car by the RAC Badge and the radiator cap, and broke it off, and probably also damaged the radiator.

Part of the wages of the man in charge of the shed might be recovered by making a small charge for each car using it.

Suggestion: (1915) If it is found that any Member of the Club has taken up arms against this country or its allies, his name be at once removed from the list of Members.

Suggestion: (1915) If it is found that any able-bodied Member of this Club has not served his country when called upon in time of need, he be requested to resign forthwith.

Suggestion: (1917) That Prince Albert of Schleswig-Holstein's name be erased from the list of Captains of the Club. I believe that the feeling in the Club is strongly in favour of this being done.

Suggestion: (1917) Will the proposer of the above suggestion kindly explain how the erasure of Prince Albert's name can alter the fact that that person was (possibly unfortunately) Captain of the Club for the year 1910?

Suggestion: (30 June 1918) We are surprised to find on our return from active service that the name of an alien Prince is still on the board of Captains. We suggest that this should be remedied.

Suggestion: (1925) That a photograph of the Club Team (handicap of 4 or over) which won the Surrey Union Golf Cup be taken and hung in a prominent position in the Clubhouse.
Reply: The Committee thought it was a marvellous suggestion, but the players declined to be photographed.

Suggestion: (1930) That the Dining Room staff be 'gingered up' considerably or that the staff be increased as it is a matter requiring undue patience and skill to obtain any food or drink in a reasonable period of time.

Suggestion: The above suggestion should be expunged from this book as an undeserved and uncalled-for slur on a body that does its best to pander to the needs of Members.

If anyone connected with the Club requires 'gingering up' at the hands of the Committee, it is the writer of the suggestion above.

Suggestion: (October 1936) Suggest that steps be taken to abate the number of house flies in the Smoking Room.

Suggestion: (1937) Suggest the Club provide an anti-aircraft gun near the 9th green (signed — Mr Smart).

Suggestion: (1937) Would suggest that General Grant be asked for plans to provide Mr Smart with a portable concrete fort, fully-equipped!

Suggestion: (1948) That no Members or their friends be allowed on the Clubhouse premises without a tie. That only a Member's family should be allowed to lunch. That ladies should not be admitted in trousers.

Suggestion: (1951) In order to overcome the objection of Lady Associate Members and wives looking into the bar from the passage, it is suggested that frosted glass be put in all lower frames.

Reply: This is receiving attention.

Suggestion: (1953) That the Autumn Meeting be postponed so as not to clash with the Ryder Cup Match.

Reply: Under Rule 24, we cannot change the date.

Suggestion: It having been rumoured that a ladies' dining room, etc., has been suggested as an annexe to the men's Club, we the undersigned most emphatically disagree with the whole idea and wish the Club to remain as now — a purely men's Club. A postcard referendum should be made.

There followed 30 signatures — filling the page. At the bottom in block caps someone wrote 'PLENTY MORE ROOM OVERLEAF!' Overleaf appeared another 45 signatures.

Suggestion: There has been a nail in the gulley of the third urinal from the end for the last four weeks. In the high standards of this Club, it will have been cleaned and replaced daily. I suggest it is not replaced next time!

Reply: The continuing lavatorial vigilance and the close observations on the degree of cleanliness are much appreciated, especially apparently by the person who lost his nail. It's been collected!

Suggestion: Members generally are worried that the flag is never flown close-hauled, because the fair lead holding the sheath is inadequate for the splice on the halyard to be hauled home, thus causing unnecessary damage to the flag, apart from being unsightly.

Suggestion: That the Club provide each caddie with a daily bowl of soup during the winter months.

Reply: The Committee are of the opinion that sufficient is already being done for the caddies.

Suggestion: The chef can't even cook rice — can we not improve on this? A new chef perhaps?

Reply: It is regretted that the chef was away on a cooking course on the day in question!

Suggestion: Please — either more sand in the practice bunker, or less stones.

After a heavily crossed-out suggestion, the writer enters beneath, 'I apologise for the above mess, but humbly suggest that a "let-off steam" book be introduced so that any Member who is provoked beyond reason can write abusively.'

Suggestion: We the undersigned are concerned at the amount of 'clearance' that has been done on the course — firstly, without consulting the Members, and secondly, without any apparent benefit to the course. The character of several holes has been altered. Are we to destroy natural growth that has taken years to mature?

Reply: Only scrub, brambles and etc. have been removed. There is a considerable amount of replanting scheduled and we would be grateful if Members would reserve their comments until the work is complete. Signed — J. Hooper-Long. Chairman, Greens Committee.

Suggestion: Hooper-Long writes in his reply to the previous suggestion, 'only scrub, brambles and etc. have been removed'. It is the 'and etc.'

that Members are concerned about. 'And etc.' is many hundreds of fully mature trees; 'and etc.' is merging the 3rd with the other course; 'and etc.' includes merging the 6th with the 12th; 'and etc.' has resulted in the 2nd being coupled with the 17th; 'and etc.' has meant that much screening not involving forestry has been removed.

Hooper-Long writes, 'We would be grateful if Members would reserve their comments until the work is complete.' TOO LATE! Trees take forty years to grow. Members are happy to see pure forestry, but do not wish the character of the course changed — especially, individual holes should not be merged with holes adjoining. Could the Committee please ensure that Members are fully informed of all further changes that are proposed, that forestry continue, and that course alterations are only undertaken with the knowledge and approval of the Members.

Suggestion: May I suggest that if the new Club Director be an existing Member that he be called 'Sir' by the rank and file?

Reply: 'Sir', amongst other things, is used as a 'vocative in addressing any male whose name is unknown to the speaker' (Concise Oxford Dictionary, 4th Edition). In such circumstances, it would be appropriate so to address the Club Director and the courtesy would be reciprocated. It is assumed that the use of the word 'Sir' as a titular prefix is not being suggested.

Suggestion: That the Suggestion Book shelf should be adjusted so that bottles and glasses slide inwards instead of floorwards.

Suggestion: The watering system costs a fortune. Why can it not be used? The greens on both courses would do Portland Cement proud! In view of the fact that £90,000 has been spent on a new watering system would the Committee tell us why our greens are a credit to Portland Cement?

Suggestion: The appearance of the publication *Playboy* in the Club has caused a lot of pleasure to the older Members. In view of this, I suggest that the Club should take it regularly.

Suggestion: My information is obviously second hand, but I am reliably informed by several Lady Members that the surfaces of their loo seats in their Locker Room are so highly polished that they would serve as a nursery slope for the next spring skiing championships!

Reply: The House Committee assembled in the Ladies' Locker Room to view the problem. No immediate action they felt was necessary, but the problem will be kept under constant surveillance.

Suggestion: Today, 25 April, the course was in a deplorable state — the greens resembled Borneville salt flats. Have we forgotten that the watering system exists?

Suggestion: Some of us were irritated on a Friday to have a society in the Men's Bar at 6 p.m. with prize-giving and *loud* clapping.

Suggestion: Many members have been 'brainwashed' into accepting the fact that they must 'tee off between 12 and 2' to avoid inconveniencing Societies of 'visiting firemen'. Starting in a threesome at 4.20 p.m. I ran up against the behinds of a singularly unattractive group on the 3rd hole. I am fully aware that the income from societies is considered to be of prime importance, BUT what the F... is the point of paying dues, only to be allowed to be a second-class citizen?

Suggestion: The Locker Rooms would look less institutional if the plastic shoe horns were *not* tied by lengths of string to the benches. How many members or guests are going to 'filch' plastic shoe horns?

Reply: Unhappily, shoe horns do get stolen. A more attractive and more effective method of securing shoe horns will be found.

Suggestion: In this modern permissive machine age with our lives governed by electronic computers or digital calculators, we human beings must reluctantly bow before the wondrous dictates of science, particularly those few of us weirdies who were made to study Latin and Greek. Therefore it is with some trepidation that I beg to call to the Club Director's attention the fact that I have twice recently been comprehensively drowned by the changing gyrations of the latest watering system, whose powerful swirling jets are far too quick for my podgy little figure whenever I try to remove my ball from the watery area that had not long before been a putting green. Perhaps at 2.15 p.m. or 7.30 p.m. on a dry summer's afternoon or evening my opponent and I, having listened to the exhortations from our Government to save bath water, should have taken a communal shower beneath its eddying torrents. If not, could the system's time switches be redirected to cast their badly-needed water only at various moments during the hours of darkness, for instance, between 10 p.m. and 3 a.m.

Suggestion: I find that some greens are harder to bounce on than others — could this be regulated?

Suggestion: The dog situation on the course at weekends has now reached epidemic proportions. If Members are unable to train their dogs so that they stay with the match in which their owner is participating, may I suggest that they should be kept on a lead. Yesterday, play in my game was interrupted by a case of rape on the 3rd green, indecent assault on the 12th and a damned good fight on the 15th! As far as I know, none of the dogs had paid green fees!

Reply: Well-behaved dogs have always been welcome at the Golf Club, except on competition days. Poorly behaved or immoral ones should be reported to the Club Secretary!

Suggestion: Could the Committee look at the Suggestion Book?

MOUNTAIN RULES-MOUNT MITCHELL

If you ever ask Ben Wright, the CBS golf commentator and journalist known for his pithy articles in the *Financial Times*, which is his favourite golfing retreat he would likely as not tell you that it is the Mount Mitchell Country Club, near Burnsville, North Carolina. Gently-contoured pasture and woodland bisected by creeks and punctuated by ponds in the cove are surrounded on three sides by towering wooded mountains. Ben is so fond of the area he bought a weekend home right on the edge of the 14th green. Mount Mitchell is a splendid place but bear in mind that if you are ever fortunate enough to go there it is highly unlikely that you'll be allowed to play under Mountain Rules!

These clearly state:

A ball rolling or landing in a bunker may be played if the golfer feels he is in need of practice. If a player elects to practise, no stroke other than the first one in the bunker shall be counted. Should the ball fail to emerge after the making of that first stroke, faulty design of the bunker is deemed

amply demonstrated and the player is not penalised for such a defect in construction.

All shots which curve into the rough on the right or the left shall be returned to the fairway at the furthest point of flight or roll, since this curvature is frequently an uncontrollable mechanical phenomenon resulting from friction between the club face and the ball.

A ball striking a tree while in flight shall be considered not to have struck said tree, unless the player making the shot declares it was deliberately planned. In this case, play shall cease while partners congratulate him. But if a player attests it was in no sense of intention to strike the tree, he shall be permitted to estimate the distance his ball would have travelled and play his next shot from that position.

There is no such thing as a lost ball. It is somewhere on the course and will eventually be picked up by someone. Therefore, there shall be no penalty for a lost ball and upon completion of the round, a player should apply for restitution to the club pro, who always has a large supply on hand.

A ball putted that rims the cup and stays out shall be deemed to have dropped, since the occurrence is contrary to the laws of gravity.

In arriving at judgement of ground under repair the player may toss a coin. If it falls to earth, the ground may be considered ground under repair.

A putted ball which reaches the brink of the cup and hangs there for want of an extra roll shall be deemed to have dropped, provided the player indicates by body contortions, gestures and words that he was genuinely desirous of this result.

Quote
Mark McCormack: 'A verbal contract isn't worth the paper it's written on.'

RICHMOND GOLF CLUB

Temporary rules 1940

1 Players are asked to collect bomb and shrapnel splinters to save these causing damage to the mowing machines.

2 In competitions, during gunfire or while bombs are falling, players may take cover without penalty for ceasing play.

3 The positions of known delayed-action bombs are marked by red flags at a reasonably, but not guaranteed, safe distance therefrom.

4 Shrapnel and/or bomb splinters on the fairways, or in bunkers within a club's length of a ball, may be removed without penalty, and no penalty shall be incurred if a ball is thereby caused to move accidentally.

5 A ball moved by enemy action may be replaced, or if lost or destroyed, a ball may be dropped not nearer the hole without penalty.

6 A ball lying in a crater may be lifted and dropped not nearer the hole, preserving the line to the hole without penalty.

7 A player whose stroke is affected by the simultaneous explosion of a bomb may play another ball from the same place. Penalty one stroke.

Having heard of these Rules, Dr Goebbels announced on German radio:
'By means of these ridiculous reforms, the English snobs try to impress the people with a kind of pretended heroism. They can do so without danger, because, as everyone knows, the German Air Force devotes itself only to the destruction of military targets and objectives of importance to the war effort.'

FINALLY, FROM THE ARMCHAIR

I'd like, if I may, to tell you this very funny story, ... about this frightfully snobbish golf club just up the road. Now I've no idea who put the rumour about that I don't like the Secretary. That's quite absurd...I have a very soft spot for him — Goodwin Sands.

Anyway, before I start this story, I would like to tell you a little bit about our club. There are some wonderful trees on the course. Well...there were, until they got Dutch Elm Disease. Then the clubhouse door got it and that's not a pretty sight — standing there, watching your knocker falling off. And I don't mind telling you that with this Dutch Elm Disease, nothing is sacred, even our Secretary's wooden leg started to warp. And in case you're wondering why Mr Morris has a wooden leg; he was camping out in Indian country when the Battle of Little Big Horn started and he went over to complain about the noise. No, no, that isn't actually quite true and, in fairness to Mr Morris, he is extremely efficient. He once forbade his three office secretaries to look out of the window in the morning.... This was so they'd have something to do in the afternoon. No, no, I'm kidding. I must be fair to the girls — they are very good really. I once asked one of them for a fibre tip, and she told me to eat more prunes.

Incidentally, after an incident involving Mr Morris, there is growing concern at the club over the height of the clubhouse furniture. Yesterday, following a committee meeting, he went into the Dining Room and inadvertently tabled his amendments.

But, I would have to admit, our clubhouse is a bit cramped. Every time the newspaper arrives, the Head Steward goes flying out of the back window. And the garden at the back is a bit overgrown. Not long ago , the Stewardess was hanging out her washing and three Japanese soldiers came out and surrendered.

But, I'm digressing again. This club up the road had its annual ball last week. Now, I enjoy these occasions as much as anyone, but the problem is that when I am dancing with a tall lady, not only can I not see where I am going, but I can't hear the band either. Anyway, at this ball, an old dowager decided to do a streak across the ballroom. One elderly member said to another:

'I say, wasn't that Felicity Montague-Benton?'

And the other said, 'Yes, I do believe it was. Did you happen to notice what she was wearing?'

The first replied, 'No, not exactly, but whatever it was, it certainly needed ironing.'

But we do have some very nice members. Take Horace Sprigg, the local Tax Inspector. At a recent fire at his office, firemen got the blaze under control before any real good was done. Then there's Sir Fabian Hine, the famous auctioneer. He had a grave disappointment last week, when the whole of his private collection went under the hammer. But we do have some really nice staff at the club. Our pro is a young Irishman. Mind you, he'd been watching too many American tournaments and felt that he had to have a pair of crocodile shoes. They were so expensive in London that he decided it would be cheaper to go to Africa to get a pair. The trouble was when he eventually reached the River Ngombo, which is notorious for crocodiles, he found that none of the crocodiles was wearing any.

Then, there's our chef, who is not one of the greatest cooks. At breakfast time, he still has to look up the ingredients for a boiled egg. Last week he made a cottage pie and the council had it condemned.

By the way, I was out on the course yesterday with my new clubs — I found them in a cornflakes packet — and I must admit, they have improved my game. I needed a 4 at the last to win the Monthly Medal, and I must confess I haven't been that nervous since I found myself in the gents with Shakin' Stevens. Anyway, I won the Medal and even received a congratulatory telegram. The cable read, 'Congratulations. If you're not the best putter in the club, I'm a Dutchman. Hans van Gelder, Amsterdam.'

But the whole point of this story was to tell you about this snobbish golf club down the road. One of our most respected members, Colonel Nithington Durge, went to see the Secretary there to try to get a round. Now, I would not accuse their Secretary of being a snob, but would you believe it — he asked our Colonel for his entire background before he'd let him play.

The Colonel stuck out his chest and replied, 'Handicap — 1. My school was Marlborough College, followed by Cambridge where I received an Honours Degree, then, of course, the Brigade of Guards, followed by the Foreign Office. In the War, DFC, DSO and Bar, before returning to the Foreign Office ...'

'Very well,' interrupted the Secretary. 'You can have a quick nine holes.'